PRACTICE BOOK

VOYAGES
IN ENGLISH
GRAMMAR AND WRITING

8

LOYOLAPRESS.

Cover Design: Judine O'Shea
Cover Art: Pablo Bernasconi
Interior Design: Think Book Works
Editor: Pamela Jennett

ISBN-13: 978-0-8294-2833-9
ISBN-10: 0-8294-2833-X

LOYOLA PRESS.
3441 N. Ashland Avenue
Chicago, Illinois 60657
(800) 621-1008
www.loyolapress.com

19 20 21 22 23 24 25 26 27 LSC 15 14 13 12 11 10 9 8 7

Contents

GRAMMAR

SECTION 1—Nouns
Daily Maintenance 1
1.1 Singular and Plural Nouns 3
1.2 More Singular and Plural Nouns 4
1.3 Nouns as Subjects and Subject Complements 5
1.4 Nouns as Objects and Object Complements 7
1.5 Appositives 9
1.6 Possessive Nouns 10

SECTION 2—Adjectives
Daily Maintenance 11
2.1 Descriptive Adjectives, Position of Adjectives 13
2.2 Demonstrative, Interrogative, and Indefinite Adjectives 14
2.3 Comparative and Superlative Adjectives 16
2.4 *Few* and *Little* 17
2.5 Adjective Phrases and Clauses 18

SECTION 3—Pronouns
Daily Maintenance 20
3.1 Person, Number, and Gender of Pronouns 23
3.2 Subject Pronouns 25
3.3 Object Pronouns 26
3.4 Pronouns After *Than* or *As* 27
3.5 Possessive Pronouns and Adjectives 28
3.6 Intensive and Reflexive Pronouns 30
3.7 Agreement of Pronouns and Antecedents 31
3.8 Interrogative and Demonstrative Pronouns 32
3.9 Relative Pronouns 34
3.10 Indefinite Pronouns 36
3.11 Agreement with Indefinite Pronouns 37

SECTION 4—Verbs
Daily Maintenance 38
4.1 Principal Parts of Verbs 41
4.2 Transitive and Intransitive Verbs 42
4.3 Troublesome Verbs 43
4.4 Linking Verbs 45
4.5 Active and Passive Voices 46
4.6 Simple, Progressive, and Perfect Tenses 47
4.7 Indicative, Imperative, and Emphatic Moods 48

4.8 Subjunctive Mood 49
4.9 Modal Auxiliaries 50
4.10 Agreement of Subject and Verb—Part I 51
4.11 Agreement of Subject and Verb—Part II 52

SECTION 5—Verbals
Daily Maintenance 54
5.1 Participles 57
5.2 Placement of Participles 59
5.3 Gerunds as Subjects and Subject Complements 61
5.4 Gerunds as Objects and Appositives 62
5.5 Possessives with Gerunds, Using *-ing* Verb Forms 63
5.6 Infinitives as Subjects and Subject Complements 64
5.7 Infinitives as Objects 65
5.8 Infinitives as Appositives 66
5.9 Infinitives as Adjectives 67
5.10 Infinitives as Adverbs 68
5.11 Hidden and Split Infinitives 69

SECTION 6—Adverbs
Daily Maintenance 71
6.1 Types of Adverbs 73
6.2 Interrogative Adverbs and Adverbial Nouns 74
6.3 Comparative and Superlative Adverbs 76
6.4 *As . . . As, So . . . As,* and *Equally* 77
6.5 Adverb Phrases and Clauses 79

SECTION 7—Prepositions
Daily Maintenance 81
7.1 Single and Multiword Prepositions 83
7.2 Troublesome Prepositions 84
7.3 Words Used as Adverbs and Prepositions 85
7.4 Prepositional Phrases as Adjectives 86
7.5 Prepositional Phrases as Adverbs 87
7.6 Prepositional Phrases as Nouns 88

SECTION 8—Sentences
Daily Maintenance 90
8.1 Kinds of Sentences 93
8.2 Adjective and Adverb Phrases 94
8.3 Adjective Clauses 95
8.4 Restrictive and Nonrestrictive Clauses 96
8.5 Adverb Clauses 98

8.6 Noun Clauses as Subjects   99
8.7 Noun Clauses as
Subject Complements   101
8.8 Noun Clauses as Appositives   103
8.9 Noun Clauses as Direct Objects   104
8.10 Noun Clauses as Objects
of Prepositions   105
8.11 Simple, Compound, and
Complex Sentences   106

**SECTION 9—Conjunctions
and Interjections**
Daily Maintenance   107
9.1 Coordinating Conjunctions   109
9.2 Correlative Conjunctions   110
9.3 Conjunctive Adverbs   111
9.4 Subordinate Conjunctions   113
9.5 Troublesome Conjunctions   114
9.6 Interjections   116

**SECTION 10—Punctuation
and Capitalization**
Daily Maintenance   117
10.1 Periods and Commas   119
10.2 Exclamation Points, Question Marks,
Semicolons, and Colons   120
10.3 Quotation Marks and Italics   121
10.4 Apostrophes, Hyphens, and Dashes   122
10.5 Capitalization   123

SECTION 11—Diagramming
Daily Maintenance   124
11.1 Simple Sentences   127
11.2 Appositives   128
11.3 Compound Sentences   129
11.4 Compound Sentence Elements   130
11.5 Participles   131
11.6 Gerunds   132
11.7 Infinitives   133
11.8 Adjective Clauses   134
11.9 Adverb Clauses   135
11.10 Noun Clauses   136
11.11 Diagramming Practice   137

WRITING

CHAPTER 1—Personal Narratives
Lesson 1 What Makes a Good Personal
Narrative?   138
Lesson 2 Introduction, Body, and Conclusion   139
Lesson 3 Time Lines   140
Lesson 4 Varied Sentences   141
Lesson 5 Exact Words   142

CHAPTER 2—How-to Articles
Lesson 1 What Makes a Good How-to Article? 143
Lesson 2 Making Instructions Clear
and Concise   144
Lesson 3 Revising Sentences   145
Lesson 4 Roots   146
Lesson 5 Dictionary   147

CHAPTER 3—Business Letters
Lesson 1 What Makes a Good
Business Letter?   148
Lesson 2 Purpose and Tone   149
Lesson 3 Adjective and Adverb Clauses   150
Lesson 4 Compound Words
and Clipped Words   151
Lesson 5 Writing Tools   152

CHAPTER 4—Descriptions
Lesson 1 What Makes a Good Description?   153
Lesson 2 Organization   154
Lesson 3 Graphic Organizers   155
Lesson 4 Thesaurus   156
Lesson 5 Figurative Language   157

CHAPTER 5—Expository Writing
Lesson 1 What Makes a Good
Expository Essay?   158
Lesson 2 Fact and Opinion   159
Lesson 3 Evaluating Web Sites   160
Lesson 4 Noun Clauses   161
Lesson 5 Prefixes   162

CHAPTER 6—Persuasive Writing
Lesson 1 What Makes Good
Persuasive Writing?   163
Lesson 2 Voice and Audience   164
Lesson 3 Advertisements   165
Lesson 4 Transition Words   166
Lesson 5 Suffixes   167

CHAPTER 7—Creative Writing: Plays
Lesson 1 What Makes Good Playwriting?   168
Lesson 2 Play Structure and Format   169
Lesson 3 Dialogue, Monologue, and Asides   170
Lesson 4 Idioms, Slang, and Jargon   171
Lesson 5 Free Verse   172

CHAPTER 8—Research Reports
Lesson 1 What Makes a Good
Research Report?   173
Lesson 2 Research and Organization   174
Lesson 3 Citing Sources   175
Lesson 4 Reference Tools   176
Lesson 5 Multiple-Meaning Words   177

SECTION 1   Daily Maintenance

1.1 **My class visited the science museum on Tuesday.**
1. What is the simple predicate of the sentence?   _____
2. What tense is the verb?   _____
3. What is the complete subject of the sentence?   _____
4. Which word is a preposition?   _____
5. Diagram the sentence here.

1.2 **The chefs are preparing a sumptuous feast.**
1. What is the simple predicate of the sentence?   _____
2. What tense is the verb?   _____
3. What is the simple subject of the sentence?   _____
4. Which word is a descriptive adjective?   _____
5. Diagram the sentence here.

1.3 **Evan's mom will send his friends invitations to the party.**
1. What is the prepositional phrase?   _____
2. Which word is a possessive noun?   _____
3. What is the object of the verb?   _____
4. What is the indirect object?   _____
5. Diagram the sentence here.

1.4 **The play will have ended by nine.**
1. What is the simple predicate of the sentence? _____
2. What tense is the verb? _____
3. What is the complete subject of the sentence? _____
4. Which word is a preposition? _____
5. Diagram the sentence here.

1.5 **Chad and Chris are the tallest players on the basketball team.**
1. Is this sentence declarative or interrogative? _____
2. Is the subject simple or compound? _____
3. Which word is a superlative adjective? _____
4. What kind of verb is *are*? _____
5. Diagram the sentence here.

1.6 **My older brothers washed the car and mowed the lawn.**
1. Is the subject or the predicate compound? _____
2. Are the verbs regular or irregular? _____
3. What are the objects of the verbs? _____
4. Which word is a conjunction? _____
5. Diagram the sentence here.

1.1 Singular and Plural Nouns

Most **singular nouns** form plurals by adding *-s* or *-es*, or by changing *y* to *i* and adding *-es*. Some **plural nouns** have special forms that must be checked in a dictionary, and some words have the same singular and plural forms.

Write the plural form of each noun.

1. fox _____
2. holiday _____
3. colander _____
4. salary _____

5. pea _____
6. potato _____
7. itch _____
8. louse _____

Underline the singular nouns. Then write the plural form of the noun. Use a dictionary if necessary.

9. The officer was sworn in by reciting an oath. _____
10. The moose ran faster than the wolf anticipated. _____
11. I like studying at the library because I go with a friend. _____
12. The woman who lives next to us is kind and generous. _____
13. I wondered how it happened that one antenna was missing. _____
14. He saw a mouse scamper under the box. _____
15. At the oasis the nomad refreshed his camels. _____
16. Each hoof of a horse needs to be cleaned regularly. _____
17. Our players' situation looked grim as a minute ticked away. _____
18. A lullaby may endure as a most comforting sound. _____
19. Both my uncle and my niece have never ridden a bus. _____
20. Not long ago, using a cell phone seemed pure folly. _____
21. The fisherman saw a flash as a trout swam by. _____

Write one sentence that uses the plural forms of each noun pair.

22. hairbrush, style

_____

23. larva, species

_____

For additional help, review pages 2–3 in your textbook or visit www.voyagesinenglish.com.

Section 1 • 3

1.2 More Singular and Plural Nouns

Some **plural nouns** have forms whose spellings change before adding *-s* or *-es*. Some words have the same singular and plural forms. Plurals of compound nouns vary. Some nouns are used only in the plural form.

Write the plural form of each noun. Use a dictionary if necessary.

1. attorney-at-law _____
2. barracks _____
3. osprey _____
4. nucleus _____

5. solo _____
6. ox _____
7. tattoo _____
8. crisis _____

Circle the correct singular or plural form that completes each sentence.

9. Franklin D. Roosevelt delivered his speeches by (radio   radioes   radios).

10. We stopped two (passerby   passersby   passerbies) to ask directions.

11. The inner workings of many (saves   safe   safes) are like mechanical puzzles.

12. While vacationing in Texas, I saw (armadillo   armadillos   armadilloes).

13. I wouldn't use any more than a couple of (thimblesful   thimblefuls) of spices.

14. After so many pregame (warm-up   warms-up   warm-ups), she was starting to limp.

15. He set the garden (shear   shears   sheares) in the deep grass and lost them.

16. (Echo   Echi   Echos) demonstrate that sounds travel fairly slowly.

17. We watched a (video   videos   videoes) about the effects of melting glaciers.

18. A billion is written as the numeral one followed by nine (zero   zeros   zerum).

19. Within a week's time, a dozen (calf   calfs   calves) were born.

20. Hemingway was a (comrade-in-arms   comrades-in-arm) of Dos Passos in Spain.

21. Each of the apartments included a small (patio   patios   patioes).

Write three sentences. Include at least one singular and one plural noun in each sentence. Underline the singular nouns once. Underline the plural nouns twice.

22. _____

23. _____

24. _____

For additional help, review pages 4–5 in your textbook or visit www.voyagesinenglish.com.

1.3 Nouns as Subjects and Subject Complements

A noun can be the **subject** of a sentence. The subject tells what or who the sentence is about. A **subject complement** is a noun that follows a linking verb and renames the subject.

Underline the subject once. Underline the subject complement twice.

1. Our new science teacher is a person with a great sense of humor.
2. Cold becomes a threat when the body can no longer maintain its temperature.
3. Day-old pizza straight from the refrigerator was his favorite snack.
4. Early cell phones were bulky, weak, and expensive radio transmitters.
5. During two weeks at camp, the lifeguards gradually became my friends.
6. That half-hearted apology was no compensation for his earlier rudeness.
7. Jackie and her mother were enthusiastic participants in the marathon last week.
8. The siblings in that family are all sculptors or painters.
9. Even after Lori moved so far away, the two girls remained good friends.
10. After he finishes this school year, my uncle will become an engineer.

Write a subject complement to complete each sentence. Underline the subject and circle the subject complement.

11. Canada is _____ .
12. In short order Elizabeth became _____ .
13. Even when the concert was canceled, Maya remained _____ .
14. Armando is without question _____ .
15. The oddly named Peppi was _____ .
16. After practicing all summer, Jesse remained _____ .
17. I am probably _____ .

Write sentences that use each set of words as described.

18. subject: volcano   subject complement: disaster

    _____

19. subject: Victoria   subject complement: supporter

    _____

20. subject: yoga   subject complement: exercise

    _____

© Loyola Press. Voyages in English   Grade 8

For additional help, review pages 6–7 in your textbook or visit www.voyagesinenglish.com.

1.3 Nouns as Subjects and Subject Complements

A noun can be the **subject** of a sentence. The subject tells what or who the sentence is about. A **subject complement** is a noun that follows a linking verb and renames the subject.

Underline the subject once. Underline the subject complement twice.

1. The Great Plains are large regions of prairie land in the central United States.
2. Generally, the states north of Texas are the ones comprised by the Great Plains.
3. These arid, windswept plains were a challenge to new settlers for centuries.
4. Lack of water and wood remained a problem for Europeans.
5. The Spanish system of conquest and mission was a failure there.
6. Gold was one of the Spaniards' main objectives, and none could be found.
7. Later, Mexicans and Americans were mere invaders to Native American people of the Plains.
8. The Comanche in particular had become extraordinary horse riders.
9. This skill was a great asset in warfare on open lands.
10. These proud warriors were the equal of any mounted troops in the world.

Complete each sentence. Write if you added a _subject_ or a _subject complement_.

11. Every child on the playground was _____. _____

12. After the rain, _____ had become slippery paths. _____

13. _____ are fantastic players. _____

14. _____ are two contact sports. _____

15. A helmet and kneepads are _____. _____

16. The player's skill was _____. _____

17. In one formation the players remained _____. _____

18. _____ will be our best strategy. _____

19. Rugby in particular is _____. _____

Write three sentences with a noun as a subject and a noun as a subject complement. Then underline the subject once and the subject complement twice.

20. _____

21. _____

22. _____

© Loyola Press. Voyages in English   Grade 8

For additional help, review pages 6–7 in your textbook or visit www.voyagesinenglish.com.

1.4 Nouns as Objects and Object Complements

The **direct object** receives the action of the verb. An **indirect object** tells to whom or for what an action is done. An **object complement** renames a direct object. A noun is an **object of a preposition** when it follows a preposition.

Underline the noun used as a direct object in each sentence.

1. My mother had always kept a beautiful antique chair in the attic.

2. Former years had taken their toll though, and the upholstery was worn.

3. Secretly, my dad transported the chair to an upholsterer's shop.

4. The upholsterer showed him material consistent with the fabric of the chair's age.

5. In the next week or so, the upholsterer carefully recovered the old piece.

6. Dad spent about four hundred dollars to have the restoration perfectly done.

7. The next day our cat Andy clawed the back of the chair entirely to shreds.

8. Dad now calls Andy the four-hundred-dollar cat.

Underline the noun used as a indirect object in each sentence.

9. The postal worker brought the manager a package.

10. Rick passed Javier the ball just as the defender arrived.

11. We sent our friends invitations to the party via text message.

12. Have you ever mailed a company the wrong check?

13. Powerful computers transmit banks updated financial information constantly.

14. You gave Elena good advice about how to manage her time.

Underline the object of the preposition in each sentence. Circle the object complements. Not all sentences have object complements.

15. You might wrongly think that the Civil War was without modern technology.

16. Some of our historians consider Lee a great general but overlook Grant.

17. President Lincoln appointed Grant General-in-Chief in the mid-1800s.

18. At this time camouflage was developed for weapons and troops.

19. The first aerial reconnaissance for military purposes took place with balloons.

20. During the war Lincoln often considered his Union commanders failures.

21. To this day some people call the Civil War the worst war in American history.

For additional help, review pages 8–9 in your textbook or visit www.voyagesinenglish.com.

1.4 Nouns as Objects and Object Complements

The **direct object** receives the action of the verb. An **indirect object** tells to whom or for what an action is done. An **object complement** renames a direct object. A noun is an **object of a preposition** when it follows a preposition.

Write whether each italicized noun is a *direct object*, an *indirect object*, an *object complement*, or an *object of a preposition*.

1. Many art historians consider Georgia O'Keeffe a *minimalist*. _____

2. O'Keeffe first studied *painting* at the Art Institute of Chicago. _____

3. O'Keeffe married *Alfred Steiglitz* and moved to New York. _____

4. She later made Taos, New Mexico, her summer *home*. _____

5. The desert landscape gave *Georgia* ideas for artworks. _____

6. She is best known for her paintings of desert *landscapes*. _____

7. One composition features a cow's skull in close-up *view*. _____

8. The artist introduced *motifs* of clouds and sky in her art. _____

9. Abstract forms are central to many of her flower *paintings*. _____

10. O'Keeffe found *inspiration* in unlikely places. _____

11. She gave her *admirers* new perspectives of nature. _____

12. Some call her artwork an abstract *record* of nature's beauty. _____

Write four sentences that use each of the following at least once: a direct object, an indirect object, an object of the preposition, and an object complement.

13. _____

_____

14. _____

_____

15. _____

_____

16. _____

_____

For additional help, review pages 8–9 in your textbook or visit www.voyagesinenglish.com.

1.5   Appositives

An **appositive** follows a noun and helps identify it. An appositive names the same person, place, thing, or idea it explains. If an appositive is nonrestrictive, or not necessary for the sentence to be understood, it is set off by commas.

Circle each noun used as an appositive and underline the noun it explains.

1. My little brother Corey is about the noisiest person I've ever met.

2. Her project, an attempt to begin a schoolwide recycling program, captured our attention.

3. We should contact Miguel's coach Mr. Sanchez for a meeting.

4. Wendy traveled to London to see Buckingham Palace, one of the Queen's residences.

5. *March of the Penguins*, a French documentary, won an Academy Award in 2006.

6. My sister Maggie wrote me a long, friendly letter from college.

7. "Old Ironsides," the *USS Constitution*, is a ship more than 200 years old.

8. Our grandfather grew up during the Depression, America's hardest economic time.

9. Rock star Mick Jagger has had a career of more than five decades.

10. The first computer sold commercially, Univac I, weighed about 16,000 pounds.

11. Dr. Fredricks, a college history professor, will speak to our class tomorrow.

12. Louis Sachar's compelling novel *Holes* won a Newbery Medal in 1999.

Write *restrictive* or *nonrestrictive* to identify the appositive you circled in each corresponding sentence above.

1. _____	5. _____	9. _____
2. _____	6. _____	10. _____
3. _____	7. _____	11. _____
4. _____	8. _____	12. _____

Write four sentences that use a noun as an appositive. Make two of the appositives restrictive and two nonrestrictive.

13. _____

14. _____

15. _____

16. _____

For additional help, review pages 10–11 in your textbook or visit www.voyagesinenglish.com.

Section 1 • 9

1.6 Possessive Nouns

Possessive nouns express possession or ownership. **Separate possession** occurs when two or more people own things independently. **Joint possession** occurs when two or more people own something together.

Circle the noun that is owned or possessed by the underlined phrase in each sentence. Rewrite each sentence so that the appropriate noun shows possession.

1. Each report <u>written by Min and Juvia</u> was excellent.

   _____

2. The father <u>of McKenzie and Trent</u> is a famous writer.

   _____

3. The tree house <u>belonging to the boys</u> is over the stream.

   _____

4. The most familiar story <u>written by Charles Dickens</u> is about a boy named Pip.

   _____

5. These old leather-bound books <u>belonging to my father-in-law</u> are priceless.

   _____

6. Kayla borrowed the bike <u>owned by her best friend</u>.

   _____

7. I saw dozens of toys <u>belonging to the children</u> scattered across the floor.

   _____

8. The shoofly pie <u>made by Ben and Theo</u> won first prize at the fair.

   _____

9. The purse <u>belonging to that woman</u> was stolen at the park.

   _____

10. The laptops <u>owned by my brother and my sister</u> were cheap, but they're already obsolete.

    _____

11. Manners should be the priority <u>of every gentleman</u>.

    _____

For additional help, review pages 12–13 in your textbook or visit www.voyagesinenglish.com.

SECTION 2 Daily Maintenance

2.1 **They should store the bigger boxes in the attic.**
1. What are the nouns in the sentence? _____
2. What person is the pronoun *They*? _____
3. What kind of adjective is the word *bigger*? _____
4. What is the prepositional phrase? _____
5. Diagram the sentence here.

2.2 **The children put their toys in the hall closet.**
1. What are the nouns in the sentence? _____
2. Which noun is singular? _____
3. Which plural noun is irregular? _____
4. Which word is a possessive adjective? _____
5. Diagram the sentence here.

2.3 **The club's members unanimously elected Sheyna president.**
1. What is the simple subject of the sentence? _____
2. What is the object of the verb? _____
3. Which noun is used as an object complement? _____
4. Which word is an adverb? _____
5. Diagram the sentence here.

2.4 **The writer Robert Frost wrote many beautiful poems.**
1. What appositive identifies the word *writer*?   _____
2. Is the appositive restrictive or nonrestrictive?   _____
3. Which noun is the subject of the sentence?   _____
4. What kind of adjective is the word *many*?   _____
5. Diagram the sentence here.

2.5 **The team's success reflects the players' hard work.**
1. What are the possessive nouns in the sentence? _____
2. Which possessive noun is plural?   _____
3. What are the abstract nouns?   _____
4. What part of speech is the word *hard*?   _____
5. Diagram the sentence here.

Name _____ Date _____

2.1 Descriptive Adjectives, Position of Adjectives

A **descriptive adjective** describes the number or qualities of a noun or pronoun. An adjective usually goes before the word it describes, but it may follow. Adjectives can also be **subject complements** or **object complements**.

Underline the adjectives in the sentences. Circle the noun each adjective describes.

1. Bright, crisp days in autumn are favorites in many parts of the country.
2. Beautiful trees, red, gold, and orange, stand out against blue skies.
3. The sharp colors seem to match the clear, cool air of the new season.
4. Yet those rich tints do not suddenly appear in the chilly air.
5. What really happens is that the lush shade of summer disappears.
6. As autumn arrives, necessary sunlight and essential water become scarce.
7. Plants cease the complex process of photosynthesis by which they produce food.
8. Chlorophyll, an important chemical in the process, gradually fades.
9. As it does, lovely shades show up in the dry leaves.
10. Magenta, gold, saffron, and yellow shades are now prominent.
11. The exquisite colors, vibrant and wondrous, existed all along.

Underline the adjectives in these sentences. Write *SC* if the adjective is a subject complement. Write *OC* if it is an object complement. If it is neither, write nothing.

12. At the outset the game just seemed tiresome. _____
13. Inning after inning went by without one score by the teams. _____
14. Two excellent pitchers retired batter after miserable batter. _____
15. The situation gradually made people nervous as time passed. _____
16. The fans grew anxious as chances to score disappeared. _____
17. Announcers called the crowd jittery as the innings passed. _____
18. Finally, a batter tripled to right field in the third extra inning. _____
19. The pitcher was undaunted, though, and then struck out two. _____
20. A weak single hit to center brought home a run. _____
21. Sportswriters later labeled the game unforgettable. _____
22. For the spectators, this game was phenomenal. _____

For additional help, review pages 18–19 in your textbook or visit www.voyagesinenglish.com.

Section 2 • 13

2.2 Demonstrative, Interrogative, and Indefinite Adjectives

> **Demonstrative adjectives** point out definite people, places, or things.
> **Interrogative adjectives** are used in questions. **Indefinite adjectives** refer to any or all of a group. Some indefinite adjectives are always singular.

Underline the demonstrative or interrogative adjective in each sentence. Write *D* if the adjective is demonstrative or *I* if it is interrogative.

1. Those petunias are my sister's prize-winning flowers. _____

2. Which backpack did you finally choose? _____

3. That painting took the artist nearly six months to complete. _____

4. What idea was in your head when you named the Pomeranian puppy "Brutus"? _____

5. Which math course did you decide to take next year? _____

6. Dad asked, "Is that outfit really the one you're going to wear?" _____

7. I don't think this color looks especially good on me. _____

8. Do you believe these boys would let us shoot baskets with them? _____

9. Whose version of events seems to make sense to you? _____

10. They found those newborn kittens in a neighbor's garage. _____

Complete each sentence with an indefinite adjective from the box. Use a different word for each sentence. Then write any other indefinite adjectives that would also complete the sentence. Some sentences have only one answer.

any	all	another	both	few
many	much	several	some	more

11. Not _____ vegetables are green. _____

12. There are _____ shoes to choose from. _____

13. How _____ money did you bring? _____

14. I did not see _____ deer in the woods that day. _____

15. Here is _____ test for you to grade. _____

16. There are too _____ students in the class. _____

17. May I have _____ coins for the meter? _____

18. I would think _____ tools were necessary. _____

For additional help, review pages 20–21 in your textbook or visit www.voyagesinenglish.com.

2.2 Demonstrative, Interrogative, and Indefinite Adjectives

Demonstrative adjectives point out definite people, places, or things. **Interrogative adjectives** are used in questions. **Indefinite adjectives** refer to any or all of a group. Some indefinite adjectives are always singular.

Complete each sentence with the type of adjective indicated in parentheses.

1. On _____ surveys, gardening is high on the list of leisure activities. (indefinite)

2. _____ surveys include urban, suburban, and rural dwellers. (demonstrative)

3. In _____ way is gardening a form of recreation? (interrogative)

4. Unlike cycling or jogging, _____ pastime is not really a sport. (demonstrative)

5. Still, _____ people enjoy the benefits of fresh air and stress relief. (indefinite)

6. Gardening is good for _____ people who can't pursue rigorous activity. (demonstrative)

7. For _____ reason, gardening appeals to people of all abilities. (demonstrative)

8. People of _____ age, however, can enjoy the creativity and sense of accomplishment gardening brings. (indefinite)

9. _____ type of gardening—vegetable or floral—do you prefer? (interrogative)

10. _____ kind affords challenges and satisfaction. (indefinite)

11. _____ types also build knowledge about botany and climate. (indefinite)

12. Even _____ individuals who cannot garden outside can still grow plants indoors. (demonstrative)

13. _____ indoor gardeners focus on floral and foliage plants. (indefinite)

14. Even an indoor gardener can grow _____ types of vegetables. (indefinite)

15. _____ type of gardening appeals most to you? (interrogative)

Write five sentences that each use one of the singular indefinite adjectives.

16. _____

17. _____

18. _____

19. _____

20. _____

For additional help, review pages 20–21 in your textbook or visit www.voyagesinenglish.com.

Section 2 • 15

2.3 Comparative and Superlative Adjectives

The **comparative** degree of most adjectives is formed by adding -er to the positive form and the **superlative** is formed by adding -est. Longer adjectives use the words *more* and *most*. Some forms are irregular.

Write the comparative and superlative forms for each of these positive adjectives.

1. cool   _____
2. steep   _____
3. noisy   _____
4. beautiful   _____
5. evil   _____

6. windy   _____
7. rapid   _____
8. quiet   _____
9. bad   _____
10. likely   _____

Complete each sentence with the correct comparative or superlative form of the adjective in parentheses.

11. Talia's hair was cut _____ (short) than I had ever seen it.

12. Oregon's Crater Lake is the _____ (deep) lake in the United States.

13. Felix finds soccer _____ (interesting) than American football.

14. The climate in Antarctica is perhaps the _____ (severe) of any on Earth.

15. Our team has a _____ (good) defense than does our opponent.

16. That road was the _____ (bumpy) highway I've ever traveled.

17. A crow is often attracted to the _____ (shiny) object it sees.

18. The weather on our vacation was far _____ (bad) than we expected.

19. Sandpaper grade refers to its grit; 60 is _____ (coarse) than 100.

20. Most animals' hearing is _____ (acute) than that of humans.

21. I thought her lame excuse was the _____ (believable) thing I ever heard.

22. What is the _____ (scary) movie you ever saw?

23. Whether a dog or a cat is _____ (smart) depends on what *smart* means.

Write a sentence that uses the comparative or superlative form of each adjective. Then write the form you used.

24. anxious _____

25. light _____

For additional help, review pages 22–23 in your textbook or visit www.voyagesinenglish.com.

2.4 Few and Little

Use **few, fewer,** and **fewest** to compare concrete nouns that can be counted. Use **little, less,** and **least** to compare abstract nouns and things that cannot be counted. There are exceptions to this rule, depending on the usage.

Write _C_ if the noun is concrete. Write _A_ if it is abstract.

1. courage _____   6. money _____   11. food _____
2. sheep _____   7. hero _____   12. talent _____
3. joy _____   8. heroism _____   13. water _____
4. tea _____   9. snow _____   14. thought _____
5. evil _____   10. leaf _____   15. herd _____

Complete each sentence with the correct form of _few or little._

16. He likes _____ noise in the room when he studies.

17. _____ dairy products now come from Wisconsin than from California.

18. Carrie had the _____ mistakes on the test of anyone in the room.

19. There was _____ gold in Alaska than many people anticipated.

20. One of our team's _____ strengths was its overall speed.

21. We had the _____ preparation time of all the classes.

22. A person with _____ hope is usually a person with _____ dreams.

23. There were _____ indications that change was on the way.

24. Ben thought he had checked out _____ books than the library showed.

25. Is there _____ honor now in the world than there once was?

26. Earlier automobiles used _____ electronic technology than today's.

27. Which state has the _____ land area of any state?

28. Our old tree produced the _____ walnuts this fall of any year we've lived here.

Write one sentence using both _fewer_ and _fewest_ and another using _less_ and _least_.

29. _____

_____

30. _____

_____

For additional help, review pages 24–25 in your textbook or visit www.voyagesinenglish.com.

2.5 Adjective Phrases and Clauses

An **adjective phrase** is a prepositional phrase that includes a preposition, a noun, and any modifiers. A **clause** is a group of words that has a subject and a predicate. Adjective clauses can be **restrictive** or **nonrestrictive**.

Underline the adjective phrase in each sentence. Circle the noun that it modifies.

1. The election of 1932 was an important one for the American people.

2. People in the Great Depression sought hope, more jobs, and new policies.

3. Franklin D. Roosevelt from New York ran against incumbent President Herbert Hoover.

4. Hoover promised better times ahead; Roosevelt promised a "New Deal" for all Americans.

5. Roosevelt won a landslide in both the popular and electoral votes.

Underline the adjective clause in each sentence. Circle the noun that it modifies.

6. Roosevelt, who took office in January 1933, had a different idea of government.

7. A government that provided help and protection for people was what he had in mind.

8. His ideas, which were new at the time, generated a lot of controversy.

9. His administration started the Social Security program that many people depend on today.

10. Another program brought electricity to many places that had never had it before.

11. The Works Progress Administration, which gave government jobs to many people, constructed public buildings, projects, and roads.

Underline the adjective clause that modifies each underlined noun. Then write *R* to identify a restrictive clause or *N* to identify a nonrestrictive clause.

12. Slowly the depression that gripped the nation loosened its hold. _____

13. Roosevelt, who was easily reelected in 1936, planned further reforms. _____

14. Some people, who had never shared his views, felt that he had gone too far. _____

15. The Supreme Court, which is the nation's highest court, blocked some programs. _____

16. He responded by trying to change the number of judges that make up the Court. _____

17. That plan failed, but the president, who had convinced people he was on their side, remained popular. _____

18. He easily won third and fourth terms, which no president had ever held. _____

19. Today an amendment to the Constitution that limits terms to two leaves Roosevelt the only four-term president in history. _____

© Loyola Press. Voyages in English Grade 8

For additional help, review pages 26–27 in your textbook or visit www.voyagesinenglish.com.

2.5 Adjective Phrases and Clauses

An **adjective phrase** is a prepositional phrase that includes a preposition, a noun, and any modifiers. A **clause** is a group of words that has a subject and a predicate. Adjective clauses can be **restrictive** or **nonrestrictive**.

Underline the adjective phrases and adjective clauses. Write *P* for each adjective phrase. Write *R* for a restrictive clause or *N* for a nonrestrictive clause.

1. Our plan for the summer involved both having fun and finding jobs. _____

2. The idea that most teens goof off all the time is unfair and untrue. _____

3. Her aunt, whom she had not seen in years, never failed to send birthday cards. _____

4. He found the cell phone that he had misplaced when it began to ring. _____

5. I laugh now, but wearing those pants without a belt was a big mistake. _____

6. Research on the Internet is easy, but it is not always reliable. _____

7. Uncle Harry, who has all sorts of odd skills, is a fantastic juggler. _____

8. Sometimes people spread rumors that other hurt people. _____

9. My father's business was in Iceland, which is surprisingly warm in summer. _____

10. His hope, which he confessed to no one, was that he would become an inventor. _____

11. She saw slow and steady improvement in her tennis game as time passed. _____

12. In most sports the teams that play the best defense usually win. _____

13. My grandmother dreads the cold and snow of winter. _____

14. Irene is interested in calligraphy, which is an ancient and beautiful art. _____

15. She was not interested in my idea, but this was news that I didn't like to hear. _____

16. I thought my idea, which I'd worked long and hard to develop, was valid. _____

Write three sentences. In the first, use a prepositional phrase as an adjective. In the second, use a nonrestrictive adjective clause. In the third, use a restrictive adjective clause.

17. _____

_____

18. _____

_____

19. _____

_____

For additional help, review pages 26–27 in your textbook or visit www.voyagesinenglish.com.

Section 2 • 19

SECTION 3 Daily Maintenance

3.1 **The Statue of Liberty is a famous landmark in New York City.**
1. Which noun is used as a subject complement? _____
2. What does the subject complement rename? _____
3. Which word is a descriptive adjective? _____
4. Is the word *a* a definite or an indefinite article? _____
5. Diagram the sentence on another sheet of paper.

3.2 **Before bedtime, he gave her a cup of hot tea.**
1. What are the pronouns in the sentence? _____
2. Are the pronouns singular or plural? _____
3. Which noun is the object of a preposition? _____
4. What part of speech is the word *hot*? _____
5. Diagram the sentence on another sheet of paper.

3.3 **Many Japanese commuters often travel on high-speed trains.**
1. Which word is a proper adjective? _____
2. Which noun can also be used as a verb? _____
3. Which word is an adverb? _____
4. Which word is an indefinite adjective? _____
5. Diagram the sentence on another sheet of paper.

3.4 **This office has less space than that office.**
1. What are the demonstrative adjectives? _____
2. Which word is a comparative adjective? _____
3. Which noun does it modify? _____
4. Is this noun concrete or abstract? _____
5. Diagram the sentence on another sheet of paper.

3.5 **These phones have fewer features than those phones.**
1. What are the demonstrative adjectives? _____
2. Which word is a comparative adjective? _____
3. Which noun does it modify? _____
4. Is this noun concrete or abstract? _____
5. Diagram the sentence on another sheet of paper.

3.6 **Every student in Mr. Lang's class must complete a research project.**
1. Which word is an indefinite adjective? _____
2. Is this word singular or plural? _____
3. Which adjective can also be used as a noun? _____
4. What is the verb phrase? _____
5. Diagram the sentence on another sheet of paper.

3.7 **After the debate, whose arguments seemed more persuasive?**
1. What kind of adjective is *whose*? _____
2. Which word is an abstract noun? _____
3. Which word is used as a subject complement? _____
4. What part of speech is *more*? _____
5. Diagram the sentence on another sheet of paper.

3.8 **Jan's and Val's cookies are good, but mine are better.**
1. What are the adjectives in the sentence? _____
2. Which word is a comparative adjective? _____
3. Which nouns show possession? _____
4. Do they show separate or joint possession? _____
5. Diagram the sentence on another sheet of paper.

3.9 **The dress with pink flowers is my favorite.**
1. Which noun is used as a subject complement?   _____
2. What is the prepositional phrase?   _____
3. Is it used as an adverb or an adjective?   _____
4. Which noun can also be used as a verb?   _____
5. Diagram the sentence on another sheet of paper.

3.10 **Ava showed me the kimono that she bought in Japan.**
1. How is *that* used in the sentence?   _____
2. Which words are used as an adjective clause?   _____
3. Is the clause restrictive or nonrestrictive?   _____
4. Which noun does the adjective clause modify?   _____
5. Diagram the sentence on another sheet of paper.

3.11 **The Grand Canyon, which is a popular tourist destination, is in Arizona.**
1. Which words are used as an adjective clause?   _____
2. Is the clause restrictive or nonrestrictive?   _____
3. Which noun does the adjective clause modify?   _____
4. Is this a common noun or a proper noun?   _____
5. Diagram the sentence on another sheet of paper.

© Loyola Press. Voyages in English   Grade 8

3.1 Person, Number, and Gender of Pronouns

A **pronoun** is a word used in place of a noun. Personal pronoun forms vary in **person, number,** and **gender.**

Underline the pronouns in the sentences.

1. Today before class Mrs. Lee asked me to run for Student Council.

2. After carefully considering the idea, I told her to add me to the list for president.

3. She gave me the nomination form and the list of campaign rules to review.

4. I asked several friends if they would help me plan the campaign.

5. We made eye-catching posters and displayed them in the main hallways.

6. The other candidate, Jeff, is the head of the debate team. He is a very persuasive speaker.

7. We worked on a speech; it must convince students to vote for me.

8. I told the student body, "You can count on me to make positive changes here at school."

9. After the election Mrs. Lee asked us to meet her so she could announce the winner: Jeff.

10. I was disappointed, but I shook Jeff's hand and congratulated him.

Write in the chart the pronouns you underlined above. List each pronoun once. Then write the person, number, and the gender, if appropriate, of each word.

PRONOUN	PERSON	NUMBER	GENDER
11.			
12.			
13.			
14.			
15.			
16.			
17.			
18.			
19.			
20.			
21.			
22.			

For additional help, review pages 32–33 in your textbook or visit www.voyagesinenglish.com.

3.1 Person, Number, and Gender of Pronouns

A **pronoun** is a word used in place of a noun. Personal pronoun forms vary in **person, number,** and **gender.**

Use the directions in parentheses to complete each sentence with the correct pronoun.

1. After dinner _____ walked along the waterfront and admired the luxurious yachts. (first person plural)

2. What did _____ enjoy most about the summer study abroad program, and would you do _____ again? (second person singular; third person singular)

3. _____ marveled at the mountain climbers and wondered how _____ could scale such heights. (third person singular; third person plural)

4. Aunt Rose sent _____ an antique cuckoo clock _____ bought during her trip to Germany. (first person plural; third person singular)

5. _____ enjoy long walks with my two dalmatians and often take _____ on hikes. (first person singular; third person plural)

Rewrite each sentence, replacing the underlined words with the correct pronouns.

6. On Saturday <u>Casey and I</u> volunteered to supervise the twins for <u>Mrs. Patel</u>.

_____

7. <u>Mr. Carter</u> showed <u>Todd and me</u> his collection of rare and valuable coins.

_____

8. <u>The collection</u> includes many coins <u>the Carters</u> brought back from trips to other countries.

_____

9. <u>Laura</u> will give <u>Alex</u> a list of supplies <u>the students</u> need.

_____

For each pair of words, write a sentence that uses the words correctly.

10. you, us _____

11. she, them _____

12. he, her _____

13. we, they _____

© Loyola Press. Voyages in English   Grade 8

For additional help, review pages 32–33 in your textbook or visit www.voyagesinenglish.com.

3.2 Subject Pronouns

A **subject pronoun** can be the subject or subject complement of a sentence. The subject pronouns are *I, we, you, he, she, it,* and *they.*

Underline the correct pronoun to complete each sentence.

1. Nick and (I   me) organized a "Save the Planet" day at our school.
2. It was (he   him) who found sponsors for the special event.
3. (We   Us) invited companies to display and present environmentally sound products.
4. (Them   They) brought a variety of green products, from lightbulbs to household cleaners.
5. A hybrid car dealer brought a car, and (he   him) explained its special features.
6. The students were enthusiastic about going green, so (they   them) asked many questions.
7. The ones who talked about recycling cans and bottles were Leila and (her   she).
8. (We   Us) learned how old clothes are recycled to make new apparel.
9. The principal could not believe it was (us   we) who organized the event.
10. Neither Nick nor (I   me) dreamed our event would be so successful.

Underline each pronoun and write whether it is a *subject* or a *subject complement*.

11. They have been preparing for the wedding since last May.   _____
12. Tonight Jean and she will teach the salsa class together.   _____
13. The student who anxiously waited to see the nurse is she.   _____
14. Robert and I purchased an energy-efficient dryer last weekend.   _____
15. The first people to reach the stranded hikers were she and Ty.   _____
16. The sly cat quickly pounced, but it did not catch the bird.   _____
17. The winner of the pizza-eating contest was he.   _____
18. The firefighters who saved the house are they.   _____
19. Trevor and Amy like Thai food, but we prefer Indian cuisine.   _____

Write two sentences for each pronoun. Use the pronoun as a subject in one sentence and as a subject complement in the other sentence.

20. he _____

    _____

21. they _____

    _____

For additional help, review pages 34–35 in your textbook or visit www.voyagesinenglish.com.

3.3 Object Pronouns

An **object pronoun** can be used as the object of a verb or a preposition. The object pronouns are *me, us, you, him, her, it,* and *them.*

Underline each object pronoun. Write whether it is used as a direct object (DO), an indirect object (IO), or an object of a preposition (OP).

1. Dad showed us a book about Ansel Adams and his photography. _____

2. As a boy, Adams struggled in school, so Ansel's father tutored him at home. _____

3. Adams loved nature's beauty and captured it in hundreds of photographs. _____

4. He conferred with other photographers and artists and shared techniques with them. _____

5. Adams befriended members of the Sierra Club and joined them on camping trips. _____

6. Adams's experiences in Yosemite left a great impression on him. _____

7. He met a young woman, Virginia Best, in Yosemite and married her in 1928. _____

8. Adams was an activist, and the protection of the environment was important to him. _____

9. Adams's work inspired me to take photographs of some favorite places. _____

Complete each sentence with the correct pronoun. Write whether it is used as a direct object (DO), an indirect object (IO), or an object of a preposition (OP).

10. I am looking for the scrapbook I made, but I cannot find _____. _____

11. Mom gave _____ a camera, and I've already taken many photographs. _____

12. My parents are talented photographers, and I've learned a lot from _____. _____

13. Sometimes my father works at home, and I help _____ in his studio. _____

14. I know how to assist my father and arrange the lights for _____. _____

15. During a long photo shoot, my mother will bring _____ a snack. _____

16. Just now she hands a plate of fruit and the missing scrapbook to _____. _____

17. My father smiles when I give _____ the recovered book. _____

18. Among these old photographs, I can't decide which of _____ is my favorite. _____

19. At our family reunion, we brought the book and shared _____ with everyone. _____

Write sentences that use each pronoun as directed.

20. me (direct object) _____

21. her (indirect object) _____

22. us (object of the preposition) _____

© Loyola Press. Voyages in English   Grade 8

For additional help, review pages 36–37 in your textbook or visit www.voyagesinenglish.com.

3.4 Pronouns After *Than* or *As*

The **conjunctions** *than* and *as* are used in comparisons and to join two clauses. To choose the correct pronoun, consider the part of the second clause that is omitted.

Underline the word to which each italicized pronoun is compared.

1. As a tutor for third-grade students, James is more patient than *I*.
2. During the week, Alyssa tutors fewer students than *he*.
3. Tamara knows more about geometry than *they*.
4. More students request the advanced math student than *her*.
5. Foreign languages such as French and Italian interest Maya more than *me*.
6. Is Lynn as prepared and organized as *she*?
7. Today Terry and Devin have as many appointments as *we*.
8. Does your brother explain word problems better than *you*?
9. Helping others satisfies me as much as *them*.
10. Students who need help with grammar request her more often than *him*.

Circle the correct pronoun to complete each sentence. Underline the word to which the pronoun is compared.

11. On the playing field, Sean is as determined as (I   me).
12. Dante has run fewer laps than (he   him).
13. Have you practiced more than (them   they) today?
14. Coach Wheeler made me do more push-ups than (he   him).
15. In the next game, I hope to score as many touchdowns as (he   him).
16. During practice the coaches are as focused as (we   us).
17. The quarterback threw Jamal more passes than (I   me).
18. Did you scout the other team? Are they as well-conditioned as (we   us)?
19. Eli was more nervous about the first game than (I   me).
20. During the first half, the fans cheered the other team more than (we   us).

Write a pronoun to complete each sentence.

21. In chemistry class, Ashley chooses Suzy as a lab partner more than _____.
22. After studying their portfolios, Ms. Anderson said Tarik paints as well as _____.
23. Both students can sing, but I think Anaya dances better than _____.
24. Mr. Wong gave Scott a bigger part in the play than _____.
25. After years of practice, Kelly plays the piano better than _____.

For additional help, review pages 38–39 in your textbook
or visit www.voyagesinenglish.com.

3.5 Possessive Pronouns and Adjectives

Possessive pronouns show possession or ownership. The possessive pronouns are *mine, ours, yours, his, hers, its,* and *theirs.* The **possessive adjectives** *my, our, your, his, her, its,* and *their* always precede nouns.

Underline the possessive pronouns once and the possessive adjectives twice. Circle the noun each possessive adjective modifies.

1. Please attempt to include a sense of perspective in your artistic composition.

2. My painting has pentimenti, changes in the work as it is being done. Can you see them?

3. Her artwork is the statue of a man on a horse. Isn't it beautiful?

4. Its cast cracked and ruined her first try. She had to start all over.

5. Is this painting yours too? I think it is much better than your first attempt.

6. I don't see their gouache compositions, but the black-and-white drawings are theirs.

7. These two statues are mine, but I don't think they're as realistic as my painting.

Complete each sentence with a possessive pronoun or possessive adjective. Underline the antecedent that provides a clue to the correct choice.

8. Let's go to Carlos's house. _____ house is the blue one on the corner.

9. I really like Amy's new haircut. _____ style is very fashionable.

10. When President Obama took office, my uncle went to _____ inauguration.

11. Lydia wants to be a professional soccer player. That kick of _____ is truly amazing.

12. Sonda's skateboard is the blue one. _____ board has the new type of wheels.

13. The babies' names are Mary and Helen. _____ parents named them after _____ grandparents.

14. The shirt is mine. I gave him _____ shirt because he spilled cocoa on _____.

Complete each sentence with an appropriate possessive pronoun.

15. Those bikes are not _____. They are _____.

16. That bike is _____, but it was damaged after my accident last week.

17. Bring _____, and I will make sure _____ is there.

18. Don't throw those away. She is sure that you didn't know they are _____.

19. The spotted dog is Stephanie and Jake's, and that cat is _____ as well.

20. I heard _____ is missing. We should help you look for it.

21. Justin and I completed the assignment. The one on the top of the stack is _____.

© Loyola Press. Voyages in English   Grade 8

For additional help, review pages 40–41 in your textbook or visit www.voyagesinenglish.com.

3.5 Possessive Pronouns and Adjectives

Possessive pronouns show possession or ownership. The possessive pronouns are *mine, ours, yours, his, hers, its,* and *theirs*. The **possessive adjectives** *my, our, your, his, her, its,* and *their* always precede nouns.

Use the context of each sentence to write the correct possessive pronoun.

1. The prototype is _____ . I gave the company my model so they could examine it.

2. The cello is Ryan's. There is no spare, so his mother brought _____ to school.

3. That bowl belongs to Lucky. He barks when he wants _____ filled.

4. Tai and Ray play many duets on the piano. We will listen to one of _____ later today.

5. Eden auditioned for the musical. Have you ever heard a voice lovelier than _____ ?

6. Does this jacket belong to you? Would this raggedy thing be _____ ?

7. Of all the reports, _____ was the best. Kristy and Karina did such a great job.

8. Aileen and I took first place in the competition. That enormous ribbon is _____ .

Write a possessive that can replace the italicized word or words. Then write *A* if the word is a possessive adjective or *P* if it is a possessive pronoun.

9. *Seaside Middle School's* colors are blue and gold. _____ _____

10. Have you reviewed *Robert's* book about football? _____ _____

11. The idea to paint our faces for the game was entirely *Paula's*. _____ _____

12. It's going to be freezing though, so let's bring *Alfred's* blankets. _____ _____

13. That large capacity cooler is *Katie's and mine*. _____ _____

14. The car with the "Go Cougars!" signs is *Natalie and Ron's*. _____ _____

15. Everyone can go in *Enrique's and your* car and meet us there. _____ _____

16. We are all so sure that the victory will soon be *the Cougars'*. _____ _____

Rewrite each sentence so the use of possessives is correct.

17. Ours house has lemon, avocado, and orange trees, but her does not.

_____

18. Mines is the best of the bunch, but hers recipe is also very delectable.

_____

19. Ours biggest problem is that my requires more maintenance.

_____

© Loyola Press. Voyages in English   **Grade 8**

For additional help, review pages 40–41 in your textbook or visit www.voyagesinenglish.com.

3.6 Intensive and Reflexive Pronouns

An **intensive pronoun** is used to emphasize a preceding noun or pronoun. A **reflexive pronoun** is used as the direct or indirect object of a verb or as the object of a preposition.

Underline the intensive and reflexive pronouns. Then write whether each pronoun is intensive (*I*) or reflexive (*R*).

1. I know that you yourself are an excellent skier. _____

2. The two of us taught ourselves how to use Mom's big kitchen mixer. _____

3. I myself thought that Julie, Ray's cousin, would have been a better choice. _____

4. Can you lift that piece of furniture yourselves, or do you need some help? _____

5. Aaron decided to paint the bookshelf himself, and it turned out wonderfully. _____

6. Abigail tried doing it herself and agreed that the directions were terrible. _____

7. This last weekend I decided to take myself out to dinner and a movie. _____

8. We ourselves recommend that you take West 5th Street instead of the highway. _____

9. You should congratulate yourselves for all the hard work you did. _____

10. Ricardo caught himself starting to fall asleep in class and quickly sat up. _____

11. Only he himself can make sure he is getting enough sleep each night. _____

Complete each sentence with an intensive or a reflexive pronoun. Then write whether the pronoun is intensive (*I*) or reflexive (*R*).

12. You all must prepare _____ for this weekend's camping trip. _____

13. This evening you _____ should consider studying for the test. _____

14. As we discussed, I will go to the library this weekend _____. _____

15. John excused _____ from the dinner table to study some more. _____

16. The scouts woke to find _____ camped in a foot of snow. _____

17. Maria taught _____ how to download songs to her new music player. _____

18. The dog wound _____ three times around the pole while waiting. _____

19. Kaitlin decided it would be easier to just walk that dog _____. _____

20. The storm _____ was the worst one many had seen in a decade. _____

21. Later many of us helped _____ to the free emergency supplies. _____

On another sheet of paper, write a brief paragraph about a time when you taught yourself a difficult task. Use at least three intensive or reflexive pronouns.

© Loyola Press. Voyages in English   Grade 8

For additional help, review pages 42–43 in your textbook or visit www.voyagesinenglish.com.

3.7 Agreement of Pronouns and Antecedents

> Pronouns must agree with their **antecedents** in person, number, and gender.

Circle the pronoun that matches each underlined antecedent.

1. <u>Devon and Jared</u> were late to class, but they will make up the time at break.
2. Alicia's <u>friend</u> Sue is back from Italy, and she has many interesting stories to tell.
3. <u>Troy</u> is the best athlete I know, but he doesn't want to try out for any teams.
4. I don't know why those <u>stories</u> were deleted, because I think they were well written.
5. <u>Rachel and Stella</u> gave a great presentation; all those slides were created by them.
6. Our prize <u>poodle</u> won Most Talented, but it failed to win first prize.
7. We wanted to invite <u>Ms. Washington</u>, but we didn't know how to contact her.
8. <u>Mom and I</u> realize Thanksgiving is next week, so we are cleaning the house for them.
9. The <u>mailbox</u> is next to the driveway; don't forget to check it every night.

Circle the errors. Write a correction that agrees with the underlined antecedent.

10. <u>Dwight D. Eisenhower</u> was the top American general during World War II, _____ and they were the 34th president.
11. The <u>Democrats and the Republicans</u> wanted him to run on their ticket _____ for president, but we could not both have him.
12. <u>Eisenhower</u> launched the space race and worked to end the Korean _____ War. You were widely considered among the greatest U.S. presidents.
13. Eisenhower sent troops into <u>Little Rock, Arkansas</u>. He made sure we _____ complied with new laws that required desegregation of schools.
14. <u>Eisenhower</u> married <u>Mamie Doud</u>. Together them moved 28 times _____ before Eisenhower retired.
15. <u>Mamie</u> was very proud of her Army-enlisted husband, and the adjustment _____ to this lifestyle was easy for him.
16. The Eisenhower family had two <u>children</u>, and you were both boys. _____
17. Eisenhower's oldest grandson was <u>Dwight David</u>, after whom Camp _____ David is named. They married the daughter of Richard Nixon, Julie.
18. After his presidency the couple bought a <u>farm</u> in Pennsylvania. _____ We were the first home they had ever owned.
19. Today the farm is a National Park Service <u>site</u>. They are open to _____ the public.

On another sheet of paper, write three sentences that have clear antecedents and related pronouns.

© Loyola Press. Voyages in English   Grade 8

For additional help, review pages 44–45 in your textbook or visit www.voyagesinenglish.com.

Section 3 • 31

3.8 Interrogative and Demonstrative Pronouns

An **interrogative pronoun** is used to ask a question. A **demonstrative pronoun** points out a particular person, place, or thing.

Write the correct interrogative pronoun *(what, whom, who, which)* or demonstrative pronoun *(this, these, that, those)* to complete each grammar rule.

1. This pronoun refers to people. It is often the subject in a question.   _____

2. This pronoun points out something singular that is near.   _____

3. This pronoun is used when asking about possession.   _____

4. This pronoun refers to people. It is the object of a preposition.   _____

5. This pronoun points out something plural that is far.   _____

6. This pronoun is used for seeking information.   _____

7. This pronoun points out something singular that is far.   _____

8. This pronoun is used when asking about a group or class.   _____

9. This pronoun points out something plural that is near.   _____

Complete each statement or question by adding the correct interrogative pronoun or demonstrative pronoun.

10. Are you going to the museum? Here, you might want to take _____ with you.

11. See the display over there? _____ is the finest collection I have ever studied.

12. Look in my hand. _____ are all arrowheads used by Native Americans.

13. _____ has purchased Native American pottery? For _____ did you purchase it?

14. _____ of the Native American tribes was historically the largest in North America?

15. _____ is a musical instrument often featured in Native American music?

16. Look here. _____ are the only books I have about the Oregon Trail. _____ on the shelves are about Native Americans.

17. _____ is this book titled *Westward Trails*? Is it yours?

Write a sentence using each word pair as pronouns.

18. these, those _____

19. who, that _____

20. which, those _____

For additional help, review pages 46–47 in your textbook or visit www.voyagesinenglish.com.

3.8 Interrogative and Demonstrative Pronouns

An **interrogative pronoun** is used to ask a question. A **demonstrative pronoun** points out a particular person, place, or thing.

Use the directions in parentheses to write the correct demonstrative pronoun.

1. Don't let your friends see _____ or they'll want one too. (far)

2. _____ are the only ingredients we need to prepare this casserole. (far)

3. Do you want several of _____ in the refrigerator or in the freezer? (near)

4. I washed the vegetables already, so now _____ can be finely chopped. (far)

5. _____ is always a successful recipe enjoyed by our guests. (near)

6. The chef will need _____, so put it on the counter, please. (near)

7. Choose carefully because _____ takes more preparation than most recipes. (far)

Write *who* or *whom* to complete each sentence.

8. By _____ was this fantastic dessert prepared?

9. I'm not sure _____ is responsible, but I can take a guess.

10. This box of materials were left here for _____?

11. From _____ did you hear that the community event had been postponed?

12. After such intense competition, _____ was considered the winner?

13. In your opinion, _____ do you think should have won?

14. _____ should I ask about the letter of application for next year?

Underline the demonstrative or interrogative pronoun in each prompt. Then complete the sentence, using another demonstrative or interrogative pronoun.

15. Which is your favorite music CD, _____

_____ .

16. Those are the most expensive shoes in the store, but _____

_____ .

17. That is the most ridiculous excuse I've ever heard, and _____

_____ .

For additional help, review pages 46–47 in your textbook or visit www.voyagesinenglish.com.

Section 3 • 33

3.9   Relative Pronouns

A **relative pronoun** is used to join a dependent clause to its antecedent in the independent clause. These pronouns are *who, whom, which, that,* and *whose.*

Underline the relative pronoun in each sentence. Circle the pronoun's antecedent.

1. The Chinese, whose civilization is very old, share their culture with the world.
2. Anyone who has eaten Chinese food has probably tasted snow peas.
3. Woks are special pans that are used to stir-fry food.
4. Chinese cuisine, which describes a style of cooking, is enjoyed throughout the world.
5. The Chinese invented the compass, which helped explorers keep their direction.
6. Compasses are important for people who steer ships and pilot planes.
7. The Chinese people, about whom you may have read, have many traditions.
8. Some popular Chinese games, which are enjoyed by many, go back thousands of years.
9. Diabolo, jumping rope, and spinning tops are games that are still played today.
10. Many generations, whose lives are enriched by these traditions, strive to retain their culture.

Circle the correct relative pronoun that completes each sentence. Underline the pronoun's antecedent.

11. Music, (which   that) is a form of art, is shared by all civilizations.
12. Megan, (who   whom) wants to play in the symphony, is learning the violin.
13. Steven asked Megan, (who   whom) he admires, to teach him to play the violin.
14. People (whose   who) voices are used in music could also be considered instruments.
15. The novella (that   whose) was read aloud is going to be the new school play.
16. People (who   whom) have acting experience may be chosen first.
17. Writers (whose   who) plays are published usually don't like to act.
18. The director discussed set ideas with the woman (who   whom) is designing the costumes.
19. Several designs, (who   which) were voted on by the actors, are being considered.
20. The date (that   who) was chosen for opening night is a good option for everyone.

Write a sentence using each relative pronoun to join a dependent clause to its antecedent.

21. that _____

22. whose _____

23. which _____

24. whom _____

25. who _____

For additional help, review pages 48–49 in your textbook or visit www.voyagesinenglish.com.

3.9 Relative Pronouns

A **relative pronoun** is used to join a dependent clause to its antecedent in the independent clause. These pronouns are *who, whom, which, that,* and *whose.*

Write the correct relative pronoun that completes each sentence. Underline the pronoun's antecedent.

1. The Maya people, _____ innovations are legendary, had a thriving population that predated the arrival of the Europeans.

2. Their system of writing, _____ consisted of hieroglyphs, was quite advanced.

3. Maya rulers, _____ were often depicted carrying weapons, captured and sacrificed their enemies for religious and political purposes.

4. The early Maya were farmers _____ lived in small villages scattered over the land.

5. These farmers grew cacao, _____ was ground and mixed with water and peppers.

6. The drink _____ was made from the ground cacao was unsweetened and bitter.

7. The Maya, for _____ trade was very important, crafted tools, pottery, and baskets.

Write *who* or *whom* to complete each sentence. Then write how the pronoun functions in the dependent clause.

8. The Maya kings, _____ also acted as priests, oversaw the construction of massive temples and palace complexes. _____

9. Raids were carried out by bands of warriors, most of _____ were likely nobles. _____

10. If you were a Maya citizen, these warriors were people _____ you may have avoided as much as possible. _____

11. At the bottom of Maya hierarchy were slaves _____ were criminals, poor commoners, or prisoners of war. _____

Complete each sentence by writing a relative pronoun used in a dependent clause. Circle the relative pronoun. Underline its antecedent.

12. Many Maya temples _____ are endangered due to the high volume of tourist traffic.

13. These buildings, _____, are examples of the Maya population's fine engineering skills.

14. The Maya people, _____, appear skillful and inventive.

15. Rituals and ceremonies _____ were important to the Maya.

© Loyola Press. Voyages in English   Grade 8

For additional help, review pages 48–49 in your textbook or visit www.voyagesinenglish.com.

Section 3 • 35

3.10 Indefinite Pronouns

An **indefinite pronoun** refers to any or all of a group of people, places, or things. Some indefinite pronouns are singular, some are plural, and some can be singular or plural, depending on how they are used.

Circle the indefinite pronouns. Write *S* if the pronoun is singular or *P* if the pronoun is plural.

1. Much of what we know about our universe comes from exploration. _____

2. When anyone visits a planetarium, he or she can learn much about space. _____

3. There are different exhibits, but most are related to astronomy. _____

4. There is something exciting and mysterious about the stars and space. _____

5. Among my friends, few think humans will ever live on the moon. _____

6. To me, nothing sounds more exciting than traveling in a spaceship. _____

7. Several have ideas for a rocket plane that could take anybody into space. _____

8. The designs for such a craft are complicated, but a few have been tested. _____

9. Anyone with enough money is welcome to venture into space on these crafts. _____

10. Neither of my sisters wants to go, but both my parents do. _____

Write an indefinite pronoun to complete each sentence. Then write its function.

11. Space is one place to be explored, but the ocean
    is _____. _____

12. Many have learned to dive underwater, but _____
    have gone to space _____

13. _____ of these places require artificial air to breathe. _____

14. There is an activity for _____ to do here on land. _____

15. A backcountry hike is _____ of my favorite activities. _____

16. I learned _____ about native plants on my last hike. _____

For each pair of indefinite pronouns, write a sentence that includes both words.

17. everyone, something _____

_____

18. all, few _____

_____

For additional help, review pages 50–51 in your textbook
or visit www.voyagesinenglish.com.

3.11 Agreement with Indefinite Pronouns

An **indefinite pronoun** refers to any or all of a group of people, places, or things. When an indefinite pronoun acts as the subject of a sentence, the verb needs to agree with it in number.

Underline the indefinite pronouns. Circle the correct verbs to complete each sentence.

1. April is Earthquake Awareness Month, and some (choose   chooses) to run simulation drills.

2. Nobody (is   are) left out of the event as everyone (has   have) an important role.

3. Several (has   have) already assembled teams that will provide first-aid care.

4. One (is   are) in charge, and the rest of us follow her set of procedures.

5. As you can see, much (go   goes) into the careful planning of this event.

6. Many (hope   hopes) that this preparation carries over to an actual emergency situation.

7. Only a few (don't   doesn't) know what it means to drop, cover, and hold.

8. Once someone (has   have) experienced an earthquake, he or she will not forget it.

9. (Has   Have) everybody reviewed his or her emergency plan?

10. Once you evacuate, either of the assistants can check off your group on his list.

11. No one (seem   seems) confused about the importance of this drill.

12. But with any event of this magnitude, something (is   are) likely to go wrong.

13. The key, however, is that all the participants (know   knows) how to react.

14. Some who have survived (say   says) it is important to know what to do after the event.

15. Everyone (agree   agrees) the event went smoothly, and no one (say   says) it was unhelpful.

Rewrite each sentence to correct the errors in agreement with indefinite pronouns.

16. Fire is a threat that anyone living in a forested area face.

_____

17. Many has no plan to evacuate, but everyone should know how their family will react.

_____

18. Most does not think about this situation until everything he or she owns are lost.

_____

19. Others invests the time and discusses emergency procedures with his or her family.

_____

SECTION 4 Daily Maintenance

4.1 **Return these overdue books to the library today.**
1. Is this sentence interrogative or imperative? _____
2. What is the subject in the sentence? _____
3. Which word is a demonstrative adjective? _____
4. Does the adverb indicate time, place, or degree? _____
5. Diagram the sentence on another sheet of paper.

4.2 **Mr. Knox often shows us copies of historical documents.**
1. Which word is an object pronoun? _____
2. What are the person and number of this word? _____
3. Which word is an adverb? _____
4. Does the adverb indicate time, place, or degree? _____
5. Diagram the sentence on another sheet of paper.

4.3 **The brown house at the end of the block is theirs.**
1. Which word in the sentence is an adjective? _____
2. Which word is a possessive pronoun? _____
3. What is its function in the sentence? _____
4. What are the objects of prepositions? _____
5. Diagram the sentence on another sheet of paper.

4.4 **He gives her more freedom than me.**
1. Which word is the subject pronoun? _____
2. Which words are object pronouns? _____
3. What part of speech is the word *more*? _____
4. Which word is an abstract noun? _____
5. Diagram the sentence on another sheet of paper.

4.5 **Meg and Mia like tennis, but they love volleyball.**
   1. What is the pronoun in the sentence?   _____
   2. What is the antecedent of this pronoun?   _____
   3. Which words are used as direct objects?   _____
   4. Which words are conjunctions?   _____
   5. Diagram the sentence on another sheet of paper.

4.6 **I myself cooked the turkey and baked the pumpkin pie.**
   1. Which word is an intensive pronoun?   _____
   2. What word does this word emphasize?   _____
   3. Which words are used as direct objects?   _____
   4. Are the verbs regular or irregular?   _____
   5. Diagram the sentence on another sheet of paper.

4.7 **Who left those muddy shoes on the floor?**
   1. Which word is an interrogative pronoun?   _____
   2. Which word is a demonstrative adjective?   _____
   3. Does this word refer to something near or far? _____
   4. Is the verb regular or irregular?   _____
   5. Diagram the sentence on another sheet of paper.

4.8 **Did you show them the postcard from her?**
   1. What are the pronouns in the sentence?   _____
   2. Which pronoun is used as an indirect object? _____
   3. Which pronoun is the object of a preposition? _____
   4. What part of speech is the direct object?   _____
   5. Diagram the sentence on another sheet of paper.

4.9 **These are the skis that she bought in Aspen.**
1. Which word is a demonstrative pronoun?   _____
2. Does this word refer to something near or far?   _____
3. Which word is a relative pronoun?   _____
4. To which word does the relative pronoun refer?   _____
5. Diagram the sentence on another sheet of paper.

4.10 **We rarely see anyone during our trips to the desert.**
1. Which word is an indefinite pronoun?   _____
2. Is this word a direct object or an indirect object?   _____
3. Which word is an adverb?   _____
4. What is the adjective phrase?   _____
5. Diagram the sentence on another sheet of paper.

4.11 **Every person who donates blood today will receive a red ribbon.**
1. Which word is a relative pronoun?   _____
2. To which word does the relative pronoun refer?   _____
3. Which word is an indefinite adjective?   _____
4. Is this word singular or plural?   _____
5. Diagram the sentence on another sheet of paper.

4.1 Principal Parts of Verbs

Verbs and verb phrases show action or state of being. The principle parts of a verb are the **base form,** the **past,** and the **past participle.** The **present participle,** a fourth part, is formed by adding *-ing* to the base form.

Underline each verb or verb phrase. Circle any auxiliary verbs. Write *past* or *past participle* to identify each verb.

1. Scientists discovered a volcano under the thick ice in Antarctica.   _____

2. This volcano had erupted more than 2,300 years ago.   _____

3. The volcano sprayed ash and rock across the pristine ice.   _____

4. Molten, hot lava had risen 7.5 miles above the glacier's surface.   _____

5. Over the years the debris was covered by layers of snow and ice.   _____

6. Special radar was used by glaciologists to study this volcano.   _____

7. Glaciologists found a pool of hot lava beneath the ice.   _____

8. This heat has shrunk the glacier's size over time.   _____

Circle any auxiliary verbs. Then use the base form in parentheses to write a verb to complete each sentence.

9. Howling with great ferocity, the wind _____ (batter) the walls of the house.

10. Craig and I had _____ (see) on the news that a tornado was possible.

11. The storm had _____ (fly) in more quickly than we expected.

12. Both of us watched in awe as the rain _____ (fall) heavily all day.

13. A massive tree was _____ (blow) down in front of a neighbor's garage.

14. Together we secured the house before the storm _____ (grow) worse.

15. We _____ (feel) that the safest place in the house was the basement.

16. The storm had _____ (rage) for hours, but luckily we never saw a tornado.

17. For most of the day, the sun had _____ (hide) behind the clouds.

Write two sentences for each word. In one sentence, use the past form. In the other, use the past participle form.

18. catch _____

_____

19. forget _____

_____

4.2 Transitive and Intransitive Verbs

Transitive verbs tell about actions that pass from a doer to a receiver. **Intransitive verbs** do not have a direct object. A **phrasal verb** combines a base verb and a preposition or an adverb.

Underline each verb, verb phrase, or phrasal verb and write whether it is *transitive* or *intransitive*. For each transitive verb, circle the direct object.

1. During the fall, millions of monarch butterflies travel south. _____

2. A female monarch lays approximately 400 eggs at one time. _____

3. The brilliant colors on the butterfly's wings scare away predators. _____

4. Ladybugs pick up scents with special organs on their feet. _____

5. Unlike humans, ladybugs will chew from side to side, not up and down. _____

6. Ravenous ladybugs nibble thousands of aphids from rosebushes. _____

7. Ants can lift objects 20 times their own body weight. _____

8. Many species of ants survive in various habitats worldwide. _____

9. Spiders pick up sound vibrations with fine leg hairs. _____

10. Some spiders spin complex webs that are stronger than steel. _____

11. Many spiders live in crevices and other dark spaces. _____

12. Most spiders' poisons will not harm people. _____

13. Crickets will avoid spiders, wasps, and other predators. _____

14. These insects cast off their exoskeletons each time they molt. _____

15. Over 450 species of dragonflies are found in the United States. _____

16. Contrary to the opinion of some, dragonflies do not harm people. _____

17. Dragonflies hover and dive in all directions, similar to a helicopter. _____

Write a sentence using each verb or phrasal verb correctly. Then write whether the verb is *transitive* or *intransitive*.

18. carry _____

19. count on _____

20. crawl _____

21. pick up _____

22. remove _____

For additional help, review pages 60–61 in your textbook or visit www.voyagesinenglish.com.

4.3 Troublesome Verbs

Troublesome verbs are those with similar pronunciations and spellings, but with different meanings and usage. These verb pairs are often confused.

Circle the verb that correctly completes each sentence.

1. I will (sit   set) the box in the corner of that table.

2. Please (rise   raise) the flag first thing every morning.

3. Susan requested that those people (sit   set) in the chairs by the window.

4. Ahmed will (learn   teach) me how to use the new computer.

5. (Bring   Take) this quarter's report card home for your parents to sign.

6. Jeremy will (lend   borrow) his brother's coat because he forgot his at school.

7. Did you notice the sleepy puppy (laying   lying) across my lap?

8. The campers have (risen   raised) early to start their long hike.

9. I have (laid   lain) clean towels on the counter for you.

10. In Mr. Smith's class last year, Krista (learned   taught) about the Civil War.

11. I needed to fix my bike, so Brett (borrowed   lent) his tools to me.

12. After browsing for an hour at the library, Jenna (took   brought) two books home with her.

Circle the verb's correct base form in parentheses that matches the context of each sentence. Then write the correct form of the verb to complete the sentence.

13. (rise   raise)   Maria _____ early to prepare the house for the graduation party.

14. (lie   lay)   Her sister has _____ festive red napkins at each place setting.

15. (lend   borrow) Thankfully, Jamal _____ us some CDs from his collection.

16. (sit   set)   Dad had brought in chairs and had _____ them by the table.

17. (teach   learn) Maria _____ a few dance moves from Patricia before the party.

18. (sit   set)   Carly immediately _____ in the closest chair.

19. (teach   learn) Everyone laughed when the twins _____ us that silly song.

20. (take   bring)   When the party ended, the sisters _____ the trash outside.

21. (lie   lay)   Maria _____ down on her bed, exhausted from the festivities.

Write a sentence that uses the form of each troublesome verb correctly.

22. lain _____

23. risen _____

24. raised _____

25. taken _____

For additional help, review pages 62–63 in your textbook or visit www.voyagesinenglish.com.

4.3 Troublesome Verbs

Troublesome verbs are those with similar pronunciations and spellings, but with different meanings and usage. These verb pairs are often confused.

Circle the correct base form of the verbs in parentheses that matches the context of each sentence. Then write the verb's correct form to complete the sentence.

1. (rise raise)   The team saluted as one man _____ the American flag.

2. (take bring)   Our team sponsor had _____ water bottles for everyone.

3. (teach learn) All the players have already _____ how to bunt and catch a fly ball.

4. (lend borrow) Since Lisa forgot her mitt, she _____ mine.

5. (lay lie)   Somebody had _____ several new wooden bats against the fence.

6. (rise raise)   The fans _____ up and cheered when our team finally scored.

7. (sit set)   I brushed off the dusty helmet and _____ it on the bench.

8. (lay lie)   Without a doubt, I will be _____ down and napping after the game.

Rewrite each sentence to correct the use of a troublesome verb.

9. Should I lent my neighbor some money to buy a few school supplies?

_____

10. We came in and set quietly as Mr. Carney was lying a test booklet on each desk.

_____

11. He had learned us some useful math shortcuts in algebra class last year.

_____

12. Michael bring his backpack to school this morning, but did not brought it home again.

_____

For each verb pair, write a single sentence that uses both words correctly.

13. rose, raised _____

_____

14. sit, set _____

_____

For additional help, review pages 62–63 in your textbook or visit www.voyagesinenglish.com.

© Loyola Press. Voyages in English Grade 8

4.4 Linking Verbs

A **linking verb** does not describe action but joins the subject with a subject complement. The **subject complement** is a noun or pronoun that renames the subject, or an adjective that describes the subject.

Circle the linking verb and underline the subject complement in each sentence. Then identify the complement as a noun (N), a pronoun (P), or an adjective (A).

1. Tap dance is a pattern of rhythmic beats made with your feet. _____

2. Savion Glover became famous for his amazing tap dance skills. _____

3. It was he who created a new style of dance called funk. _____

4. Audiences were enthusiastic about his energetic, pounding rhythms. _____

5. Thanks to a role on a television show, Glover became well-known. _____

6. Other dancers such as Gregory Hines felt inspired by Glover's talents. _____

7. Glover is also a choreographer who creates dances for many shows. _____

8. Because of his talent, Glover has been the recipient of several awards. _____

9. His funk style remains fresh and exciting even today. _____

Underline each verb. Write whether it is *transitive*, *intransitive*, or *linking*.

10. The school band marched around the field in a synchronized formation. _____

11. Their coordinated uniforms were bright orange and blue. _____

12. Proudly, they performed the school song for the cheering crowds. _____

13. The shouts and cheers grew louder with each additional song. _____

14. The spectators clapped enthusiastically after the performance. _____

Circle the eight linking verbs and underline their subject complements.

This morning the sky appears clear, blue, and sunny. The day

seems perfect for a beach trip. Today, however, I am a student. As I

sit here daydreaming, the air smells fresh and the sun is warm on

my skin. Even the imaginary waves sound thunderous. Suddenly

the whole class stares at me. My face grows hot. No wonder I could

visualize that beach. I guess I had been asleep.

© Loyola Press. Voyages in English Grade 8

For additional help, review pages 64–65 in your textbook or visit www.voyagesinenglish.com.

4.5 Active and Passive Voices

A transitive verb has voice. When a transitive verb is in the **active voice,** the subject is the doer of the action. When a transitive verb is in the **passive voice,** the subject is the receiver of the action.

Underline the verb or verb phrase. Write _A_ if the verb is in the active voice and _P_ if it is in the passive voice.

1. Amazing sidewalk art was created by artist Julian Beever. _____

2. His images included renderings of well-known paintings and original designs. _____

3. A variety of subjects were chosen by the artist. _____

4. Mr. Beever used colored chalk for his elaborate drawings. _____

5. First, Beever drew a miniature design of an image or a scene. _____

6. Based on this design, the artist sketched a three-dimensional picture. _____

7. In a reasonable amount of time, realistic pictures were created by Beever. _____

8. Entire sections of a city's sidewalk were filled with his art. _____

9. Then the artist recorded each work of art in a photograph. _____

10. Interestingly, the camera's view showed the best three-dimensional effect. _____

11. These magnificent photos were uploaded by the artist to the Internet. _____

12. Many fans enjoyed the Internet postings of new creations. _____

If the sentence is in the active voice, rewrite it in the passive voice. If the sentence is in the passive voice, rewrite it in the active voice.

13. Leonardo da Vinci, a man of many talents, painted the _Mona Lisa._

_____

14. The famous _Last Supper_ was also painted by Leonardo da Vinci.

_____

15. The Louvre in Paris, France, displays the _Mona Lisa._

_____

16. Notes for inventions and other ideas were written backward by Leonardo.

_____

17. The Renaissance ushered in a period of rebirth in art and learning.

_____

For additional help, review pages 66–67 in your textbook or visit www.voyagesinenglish.com.

4.6 Simple, Progressive, and Perfect Tenses

Verb forms indicate **tense**. **Simple, progressive,** and **perfect tenses** all have forms in the present, past, and future.

Underline each verb or verb phrase and write the letter to identify the tense. Then write _past, present,_ or _future_ to identify the action each verb or verb phrase expresses.

a. Simple tense   **b.** Progressive tense   **c.** Perfect tense

1. My brother studies diligently every night for two hours.   _____ _____
2. The gymnasium will be closing at nine o'clock sharp.   _____ _____
3. We are preparing for next week's competition.   _____ _____
4. The candidates have posted their signs for the election.   _____ _____
5. Our class will visit the museum at the end of the month.   _____ _____
6. John has purchased a new tire for his bicycle.   _____ _____
7. The chores will have been finished by the time I get home.   _____ _____
8. Amy will have read five books by the end of summer.   _____ _____
9. The researchers presented their findings at a public hearing.   _____ _____
10. We will be working together on the science project.   _____ _____
11. I was selling tickets for the student talent show.   _____ _____
12. The issue has been discussed at several meetings recently.   _____ _____

Write a sentence that uses each verb phrase in the passive voice.

13. will have sent

_____

14. had offered

_____

15. has solved

_____

16. had constructed

_____

For additional help, review pages 68–69 in your textbook or visit www.voyagesinenglish.com.

Section 4 • 47

4.7 Indicative, Imperative, and Emphatic Moods

Verb forms indicate mood. The **indicative mood** is used to state a fact or ask a question. The **imperative mood** is used to give commands. The **emphatic mood** gives special force to a simple present or past tense verb.

Underline the verb or verb phrase in each sentence. Then write *indicative,* *imperative,* **or** *emphatic* **to identify the verb's mood.**

1. People have been creating quilts for centuries. _____

2. Historically, quilts were constructed from bits of leftover fabric. _____

3. At one time people really did make all their clothes by hand. _____

4. Quilters often assisted one another with their quilts. _____

5. Quilting does bring friends and neighbors together. _____

6. Have you ever slept under a handmade quilt? _____

7. Gather pins, needles, and thread ahead of time. _____

8. Choose colorful cotton fabrics for the face and backing. _____

9. Two interesting quilt patterns are called snowball and log cabin. _____

10. Use a sewing machine for less time and effort. _____

Write the mood of each sentence. Rewrite indicative sentences as imperative and imperative sentences as indicative.

11. Join us for the picnic on Sunday. _____

_____

12. We are planning a trip to Chile this summer. _____

_____

13. My cousin really did eat three slices of birthday cake. _____

_____

14. Please bring the necessary supplies to class. _____

_____

15. Jana is playing varsity tennis this year. _____

_____

For additional help, review pages 70–71 in your textbook or visit www.voyagesinenglish.com.

4.8 Subjunctive Mood

The **subjunctive mood** of a verb can express a wish, a desire, or a condition contrary to fact. It is also used to express a demand or a recommendation after *that*, or to express an uncertainty after *if* or *whether*.

Underline each verb or verb phrase in the subjunctive mood. Write the purpose of each: a wish or desire (*W*), a contrary-to-fact condition (*C*), a demand or recommendation (*D*), or an uncertainty (*U*).

1. I wish I were tall enough for basketball. _____
2. If I had long legs, I could be a star player. _____
3. My mother insists that I eat healthy food. _____
4. Perhaps if I had eaten more vegetables, I would have grown taller. _____
5. I won't eat broccoli, whether it be good for me or not. _____
6. To get stronger, my coach suggests that I work out after school. _____
7. In my dreams I wish the Bulls would invite me to join the team. _____
8. I will always play basketball, whether I be seven feet tall or not. _____
9. The school board recommended that all new programs be funded this year. _____
10. Whether it be expensive or a bargain, we will take a vacation soon. _____
11. The rules require that students be earning passing grades. _____

Circle the correct verb form to complete each sentence. Then circle the numbers of the sentences that have verbs in the subjunctive mood.

12. The director said it is necessary that the cast (show   shows) up on time.
13. I wish I (was   were) on the stage crew instead of in the chorus line.
14. The stage manager doesn't require that the crew (be   are) on hand all the time.
15. I know that the stage manager wasn't angry when I (was   were) late for rehearsal once.
16. I'm going to request that I (be   am) given time off work when I'm needed there.
17. My mother considers that to be a good deed that (build   builds) character.
18. Whether I (be   am) a member of the crew or the cast, I will always do my best.
19. All cast members (be   are) required to memorize their lines.

On another sheet of paper, write about some things your parents suggest you do and what they require you to do. Use at least three sentences that have verbs in the subjunctive mood.

For additional help, review pages 72–73 in your textbook or visit www.voyagesinenglish.com.

Section 4 • 49

4.9 Modal Auxiliaries

Modal auxiliaries are used with main verbs to express permission, possibility, ability, obligation, and intention. Common modal auxiliaries are *may, might, can, could, must, should, will,* and *would.*

Underline each verb phrase with a modal auxiliary. Write whether the verb phrase expresses *permission, possibility, ability, necessity, obligation,* or *intention*.

1. During the afternoon, we may work on our science project. _____

2. My group can make a display board about our topic. _____

3. I might plan a list of jobs for each group member. _____

4. Evan and Julio will record data from our experiment. _____

5. According to the guidelines, our data must be arranged in order. _____

6. The group should have met last week at Neela's house. _____

7. Some of the research can be completed at the library tonight. _____

8. We must prepare a two-page report by the end of the week. _____

9. Our final grade will be based on our report and its display. _____

10. Our group might choose to use colorful computer graphics. _____

Use modal auxiliaries to write sentences on the topics. Use the underlined words and clues in parentheses to help you choose the correct verbs.

11. Cleaning your room (obligation, past tense)

_____

12. Borrowing a sweater (permission, present tense)

_____

13. Shopping for a gift (intention, future tense)

_____

14. Finishing a task (possibility, past tense)

_____

15. Following directions (necessity, present tense)

_____

16. Cooking a meal (ability, present tense)

_____

© Loyola Press. Voyages in English   Grade 8

For additional help, review pages 74–75 in your textbook or visit www.voyagesinenglish.com.

4.10 Agreement of Subject and Verb—Part I

A verb agrees with its subject in person and number. Special rules apply when using *don't* and *doesn't*, when *you* is the subject, when *there is* and *there are* introduce a sentence, or when phrases come between subjects and verbs.

Circle the correct form of the verb in parentheses that completes the subject-verb agreement in each sentence. Underline the simple subject.

1. Thin, small trees (bend   bends) during powerful winds.

2. (Was   Were) you living here during the Northridge earthquake?

3. There (is   are) several wildfires raging in those dry hills.

4. A good place to hide during a tornado (is   are) the basement.

5. Which American city (face   faces) the fewest floods each year?

6. Hurricanes, as well as thunderstorms, (is   are) common in Florida.

7. The overflow of rivers (create   creates) floods in some areas.

8. (Is   Are) you aware that a tsunami can follow an earthquake?

9. Alaska (don't   doesn't) get sunshine during certain times of the year.

Circle the simple subject in each sentence and underline the error in subject-verb agreement. Then write the correct form of the verb.

10. Most people doesn't know what to do during an earthquake.   _____

11. Was you able to obtain an earthquake safety manual?   _____

12. I doesn't know which state gets the most snowfall each year.   _____

13. There is several commonsense rules one should know.   _____

14. One state with historic snowfalls are South Dakota.   _____

15. There has been many hurricanes in Louisiana this year.   _____

16. Oklahoma, a Midwestern state, experience many tornadoes.   _____

17. Lightning may often strikes without warning.   _____

Complete each sentence. Be sure the subject and verb agree.

18. You always _____ at every summer concert.

19. I can't ride my bike because it _____.

20. The _____ with _____ runs _____.

For additional help, review pages 76–77 in your textbook or visit www.voyagesinenglish.com.

Section 4 • 51

4.11 Agreement of Subject and Verb—Part II

A **collective noun** usually requires a singular verb. **Indefinite pronouns** are singular and take singular verbs. Some nouns that are **plural in form are singular in meaning** and require singular verbs.

Underline each simple subject. Circle the verb in parentheses that correctly completes each sentence.

1. My mom and dad (is   are) taking us on a trip to Europe.

2. My family (travels   travel) somewhere new each summer.

3. Each of us (seems   seem) enthusiastic about a different country.

4. Another place we'd really like to visit (is   are) China.

5. Many of us (enjoy   enjoys) trying different ethnic foods.

6. Our tour group (chooses   choose) which cities to explore.

7. Sometimes the news (tell   tells) us more information about places we will visit.

8. Neither my brother nor I (have   has) been out of the United States yet.

Underline each simple subject. Then complete each sentence with the correct form of a present tense verb.

9. Each of us _____ to get new clothes for the trip.

10. My family and I _____ the first week of July.

11. The crowd _____ carefully to the tour guide.

12. The culture and language of Spain _____ interesting to me.

13. Either a travel agency or the Internet _____ helpful travel tips.

14. The Louvre in Paris _____ one of the museums we may visit.

15. Everyone _____ many new and exciting adventures.

16. Two things my dad wants to see _____ the Eiffel Tower and Big Ben.

Circle the errors in each sentence. On another sheet of paper, rewrite each sentence correctly.

17. Before vacation, many travelers copies their passports and purchases traveler's checks.

18. Lugguage take a lot of abuse, so travelers needs a sturdy set.

19. An organized traveler arrive on time and stay calm in frustrating situations.

For additional help, review pages 78–79 in your textbook or visit www.voyagesinenglish.com.

4.11 Agreement of Subject and Verb—Part II

A **collective noun** usually requires a singular verb. **Indefinite pronouns** are singular and take singular verbs. Some nouns that are **plural in form are singular in meaning** and require singular verbs.

Use the correct form of the verb in parentheses to complete each sentence. Underline the simple subject.

1. Neither my friend nor I _____ (know) how to play tennis.

2. There _____ (be) two beginner classes at the park.

3. Last year Steve and Marcie _____ (be) the only people who took lessons.

4. The instructors in the class _____ (serve) us one ball after another.

5. The game of tennis _____ (require) many hours of practice.

6. When choosing a racket, size and weight _____ (be) important.

7. The tennis team _____ (play) in tournaments during the summer.

8. Everybody on the team _____ (wear) a yellow visor, but I _____ (wear) a blue one.

Add a subject to complete each sentence.

9. _____ are practiced by the players several times each day.

10. _____ were given to each of the teams.

11. _____ seats over 1000 spectators.

12. _____ is willing to practice four times a week.

13. _____ necessitate a serious commitment of time and effort.

Write two sentences for each noun-verb pair. Use the noun's singular form as the subject in one sentence and its plural form in the other.

14. racket, break _____

_____

15. player, serve _____

_____

16. team, lose _____

_____

For additional help, review pages 78–79 in your textbook or visit www.voyagesinenglish.com.

Section 4 • 53

SECTION 5 | Daily Maintenance

5.1 **Mary herself renovated the entire house.**
1. What is the verb in the sentence?   _____
2. What tense is the verb?   _____
3. Which word is a pronoun?   _____
4. Is this pronoun intensive or reflexive?   _____
5. Diagram the sentence on another sheet of paper.

5.2 **The weary ticket buyers had waited in line for several hours.**
1. What is the verb phrase in the sentence?   _____
2. Is it a present participle or a past participle?   _____
3. What kind of adjective is *several*?   _____
4. What part of speech is *weary*?   _____
5. Diagram the sentence on another sheet of paper.

5.3 **The noisy children are playing happily in the backyard.**
1. What is the complete subject of the sentence?   _____
2. What is the verb phrase?   _____
3. Is it transitive or intransitive?   _____
4. Which word is an adverb?   _____
5. Diagram the sentence on another sheet of paper.

5.4 **These yachts are luxurious and very expensive.**
1. Which word is the linking verb in the sentence?   _____
2. Which word is an indefinite adjective?   _____
3. What does it describe?   _____
4. What are the subject complements?   _____
5. Diagram the sentence on another sheet of paper.

5.5 **This jewelry was designed by my friend Elena.**
1. What is the verb phrase in the sentence?   _____
2. Is it in active or passive voice?   _____
3. Which word is an appositive?   _____
4. Which word does the appositive rename?   _____
5. Diagram the sentence on another sheet of paper.

5.6 **Javier and I will be performing in the school play this spring.**
1. What is the verb phrase in the sentence?   _____
2. What tense is this verb phrase?   _____
3. Is the subject or the predicate compound?   _____
4. Is *I* a subject pronoun or an object pronoun? _____
5. Diagram the sentence on another sheet of paper.

5.7 **She has been working with me at the bakery for two years.**
1. What is the verb phrase in the sentence?   _____
2. What is the tense of this verb phrase?   _____
3. Which word is an object pronoun?   _____
4. How many prepositional phrases are there?   _____
5. Diagram the sentence on another sheet of paper.

5.8 **This month we are collecting food and clothing for the Red Cross.**
1. What is the verb phrase in the sentence?   _____
2. Is the verb form indicative or imperative?   _____
3. What tense is the verb phrase?   _____
4. Is the verb phrase transitive or intransitive? _____
5. Diagram the sentence on another sheet of paper.

5.9 Thirty minutes of daily exercise does improve your health.
1. What is the verb phrase in the sentence?   _____
2. Is the verb form indicative or emphatic?   _____
3. Is the verb phrase transitive or intransitive?   _____
4. What is the prepositional phrase?   _____
5. Diagram the sentence on another sheet of paper.

5.10 Include a bibliography at the end of your research paper.
1. What is the verb in the sentence?   _____
2. Is the verb form indicative or imperative?   _____
3. Which word is the direct object of the verb?   _____
4. Which words are objects of prepositions?   _____
5. Diagram the sentence on another sheet of paper.

5.11 Those students should receive recognition for their accomplishments.
1. What is the verb phrase in the sentence?   _____
2. Which word is a modal auxiliary?   _____
3. Does it express permission or obligation?   _____
4. What kind of adjective is *their*?   _____
5. Diagram the sentence on another sheet of paper.

5.1 Participles

> **Verbals** are words made from verbs to function as another part of speech. A **participle** is a verb form used as an adjective. A **participial phrase** is made up of the participle, an object or a complement, and any modifiers.

Underline the participial phrase in each sentence. Circle the noun or pronoun it describes.

1. The Pulitzer Prize, named for Joseph Pulitzer, is awarded annually.

2. These prizes, given to American writers, honor excellence in writing.

3. Having been born in Hungary, Pulitzer sailed to America as a young man.

4. He got his first journalism job, writing for a German-language newspaper, after he impressed the editors with his intelligence.

5. The newspaper, facing bankruptcy, was later offered to Joseph.

6. He developed a reputation built on hard work and smart business deals.

7. Having been a failing newspaper, *The New York World* was a success under his ownership.

8. Concerned by corruption in business and government, Mr. Pulitzer used his newspapers to expose these issues.

9. Pulitzer completed his will describing his plans for a journalism award in 1904.

10. Today 21 award categories are recognized, divided between journalism, literature, music, and drama.

11. Reading Pulitzer's biography, we can learn about the importance of perseverance.

Underline the participial phrase in each sentence. Circle the participle if it is active. Write *present*, *past*, or *perfect* to identify the tense of the participle.

12. Grinning from ear to ear, Carmen proudly accepted the gold medal.   _____

13. Selected from 10 applicants, Lee presented a speech at the ceremony.   _____

14. The geography competition, involving 50 students, was held at school.   _____

15. The team, having been awarded first place, celebrated with their families.   _____

16. Entering the contest in a magazine, I hope to win the grand prize.   _____

17. My sister, being awarded a blue ribbon, proudly stood next to her art.   _____

18. Surprised by her teammates, Lydia gazed at the Best Player plaque.   _____

19. Having lost the wrestling match, Dimitri shook hands with the winner.   _____

20. Maya hoped to win one of the prizes listed on the raffle ticket.   _____

21. Having won every game, the team went on to win the championship.   _____

For additional help, review pages 84–85 in your textbook or visit www.voyagesinenglish.com.

5.1   Participles

> **Verbals** are words made from verbs to function as another part of speech. A **participle** is a verb form used as an adjective. A **participial phrase** is made up of the participle, an object or a complement, and any modifiers.

Underline the participial phrase in each sentence. Circle the noun or pronoun it describes. Write *present*, *past*, or *perfect* to identify the tense of the participle.

1. The timid girl waiting by the door is my younger sister.   _____

2. Having been given a second chance, I recited the speech perfectly.   _____

3. The parrot, having been taught to speak, mimicked everyone.   _____

4. Fiona gazed at the sun setting over the peaks in an explosion of color.   _____

5. Kibble, having eaten the carrot, retired to the back of his cage.   _____

6. Loved by its new family, the stray dog had finally found a home.   _____

7. The river, surging through the tiny town, was dangerously high.   _____

8. Cheering loudly, Keisha watched the team score its third touchdown.   _____

9. Hit with a baseball, the window shattered into tiny shards of glass.   _____

10. Having lost the game, we realized that the team needed more practice.   _____

11. My aunt, dressed in her comfortable old apron, cooked a holiday feast.   _____

12. Having been hidden under the armchair, the kitten slept for hours.   _____

Finish the participial phrase that describes the italicized noun to complete each sentence.

13. Amazed _____, our science *class* watched a
    documentary about talking birds.

14. Some students researched about *dolphins* communicating _____

    _____.

15. Working _____, *I* tested my hypothesis about how
    sound travels from the animals to the ear.

16. The *student* sitting _____ recorded the results of my experiment.

17. Searching _____, *Carlos* discovered that some species
    of turtles do hiss when startled.

18. My lab partner and I prepared a detailed *graph* summarizing _____.

19. *Mrs. Santos*, having noticed _____, planned a field trip to the
    zoo for all science classes.

© Loyola Press. Voyages in English   Grade 8

For additional help, review pages 84–85 in your textbook
or visit www.voyagesinenglish.com.

5.2 Placement of Participles

A **participle** used as an adjective before or after the word it modifies, or after a linking verb, is a **participial adjective.** A participial phrase acts as an adjective when it describes a noun or pronoun.

Underline the participial adjective in each sentence.

1. Slithering snakes hunt for food.

2. Little light filters through the swaying trees of the canopy.

3. Chirping squirrel monkeys swing from branches overhead.

4. Many surviving species receive the protection of local laws.

5. A rain forest's covered environment is warm and moist.

6. Most laws of protection have brought about the wanted results.

7. One-third of the world's required oxygen supply is provided by rain forests.

8. Big cats, such as the jaguar, prefer to rest in hidden places during the day.

9. Thousands of species of butterflies survive among the dripping trees of the rain forest.

10. Many plants and animals seem perfectly adapted to conditions in the rain forest.

Underline the participial adjective in each sentence. Write the word it modifies. If the participial adjective follows a linking verb, circle the verb.

11. All people must remain focused on reducing, reusing, and recycling. _____

12. Many caring citizens donate time and money to conservation groups. _____

13. Some animals are endangered and should not be purchased as pets. _____

14. Don't use a large sheet of writing paper for a small note. _____

15. Harvesting companies can replace what they remove from the forest. _____

16. Groups work to end the growing threats of fire and criminal activity. _____

17. Many people are confused about the state of the world's forests. _____

Write a sentence for each phrase. Circle the participle.

18. recycling bin _____

19. vanishing forests _____

20. wasted water _____

21. singing birds _____

22. camping trip _____

© Loyola Press. Voyages in English   Grade 8

For additional help, review pages 86–87 in your textbook or visit www.voyagesinenglish.com.

Section 5 • 59

5.2 Placement of Participles

> A **participle** used as an adjective before or after the word it modifies, or after a linking verb, is a **participial adjective.** A participial phrase acts as an adjective and therefore must describe a noun or pronoun.

Underline the participial adjectives and participial phrases. Circle the noun that each modifies.

1. Mr. Zimmer displayed several baskets woven with various types of reeds.

2. The students were excited by this new project and eagerly discussed ways to begin.

3. Basket weaving, practiced throughout the world, creates functional works of art.

4. One basket, having been designed with square sides, was especially intriguing to Jenna.

5. Having watched the how-to video, the class began collecting materials.

6. Finally deciding on a design, Anna chose a swirling pattern of lines.

7. Jeffrey having learned to weave before, quickly understood what to do.

8. Weaving the reeds in and out, the students began the sides of their baskets.

9. Because the reeds can break, this project was challenging for me.

10. Each student was hurrying to complete his or her basket in the allotted time.

11. Impressed by the quality of their work, the teacher displayed the finished baskets.

12. When I told her the basket was now hers, my mom was pleased by my creative gift.

Rewrite each sentence to correct the dangling or misplaced participle.

13. Wet from the storm, I allowed our dog to come into the house.

   _____

14. Hurrying to get to class on time, the door was already closed.

   _____

15. Having been soaked in warm water, I began weaving the basket.

   _____

16. Reaching into the box, the winning ticket was selected.

   _____

17. Kate performed magic tricks for her friends, having practiced all day.

   _____

For additional help, review pages 86–87 in your textbook or visit www.voyagesinenglish.com.

5.3 Gerunds as Subjects and Subject Complements

A **gerund** is a verb form ending in *-ing* used as a noun. A gerund or gerund phrase can be used as a subject or subject complement in a sentence.

Underline the gerund or gerund phrase in each sentence. Circle any direct objects that are part of the phrase. Then write *S* if the gerund or gerund phrase is used as a subject or *SC* if it is used as a subject complement.

1. The start of our vacation is driving to the campground in Wisconsin. _____

2. Parking the camper safely is a project for the whole family. _____

3. Fishing is dad's favorite activity when he is outdoors. _____

4. Meeting other campers is one activity we all enjoy. _____

5. My brother's responsibility is gathering firewood for the campfire. _____

6. Hiking through the woods can be a chance to see animals up close. _____

7. An activity that refreshes us on a hot afternoon is swimming in the lake. _____

8. Napping beneath a shady tree was my brother's plan. _____

9. Building a fire is dangerous if safety procedures are ignored. _____

10. My special skill is cooking delicious food over the campfire. _____

11. Singing songs at the end of the day remains our favorite activity. _____

12. Our goal in the trip's end is removing every trace that we were there. _____

Circle the sentence in each pair that contains a gerund or gerund phrase. Write *subject* or *subject complement* to identify its use in the sentence.

13. Part of my job at the bakery is tasting new foods.
    At the bakery I am tasting new foods as part of my job. _____

14. Eating a granola bar is a healthy way to snack.
    She is eating this granola bar as part of a healthy snack. _____

15. Because of her hobby, Rosa was sampling exotic foods.
    Rosa's hobby is sampling exotic foods. _____

16. It hurts my teeth when I am chewing gum.
    Chewing gum is a product that is hard on my teeth. _____

17. Sipping water during exercise is a healthy habit for athletes.
    I am always sipping water when I exercise. _____

18. It was funny to see the mouse nibbling a bit of cheese.
    Nibbling little pieces is a funny way to eat cheese. _____

For additional help, review pages 88–89 in your textbook or visit www.voyagesinenglish.com.

Section 5 • 61

5.4 Gerunds as Objects and Appositives

A gerund or gerund phrase can be used as a direct object, as the object of a preposition, or as an appositive.

Underline the gerund phrase and circle the gerund. Identify how the gerund is used by writing *DO* (direct object), *OP* (object of a preposition), or *A* (appositive).

1. Apparently, Amanda loves throwing parties on the weekends. _____
2. Tanya exercises by swimming 30 laps every morning. _____
3. Min tried sketching portraits of people rather than animals. _____
4. Jared enjoys watching football on Sunday afternoons. _____
5. Many people do not like giving speeches in front of large groups. _____
6. I didn't know math skills could lead to getting so many interesting jobs. _____
7. Trey's talent, acting in the community theater, will take him far someday. _____
8. Are you the one who started using that nickname for me? _____
9. Jeremy began his research by reading books about motorcycles. _____
10. Cara and Ann had dinner after shopping for holiday gifts. _____
11. His homework plan, completing the hard parts first, will help him finish faster. _____

Complete each sentence with a gerund phrase. Then write how the gerund is used—as a direct object (*DO*), an object of the preposition (*OP*), or an appositive (*A*).

12. The softball coach demonstrated _____. _____
13. Sometimes it is easier to learn by _____. _____
14. The team practices the difficult skill, _____, every day. _____
15. I check all my equipment before _____. _____
16. At most practices one player starts _____. _____
17. Our team's best skill, _____, has helped us win many games. _____
18. On certain days I cannot stop _____. _____
19. One popular activity, _____, is good exercise. _____
20. The spectators show their support by _____. _____
21. Our shortstop made an out by _____. _____
22. The team receives snacks after _____. _____

For additional help, review pages 90–91 in your textbook or visit www.voyagesinenglish.com.

5.5 Possessives with Gerunds, Using *-ing* Verb Forms

Gerunds may be preceded by a possessive form—either a possessive noun or a possessive adjective. These possessives describe the doer of the action of the gerund.

Circle the word that correctly completes each sentence.

1. (Us   Our) visiting Alaska was the entire family's decision.

2. (Your   You) lending me this book will save me a trip to the library.

3. (Amy   Amy's) taking an earlier flight gave her more time for sightseeing.

4. I hope that (my   me) studying hard for this exam will result in a good grade.

5. (Aaron   Aaron's) researching the history project saved time for the whole group.

6. Based on the scores, (Pedro's   Pedro) dancing exceeded the expectations of the judges.

7. (He   His) performing those complicated steps with such skill amazed the audience.

8. I thought (John   John's) helping create the Web site showed his commitment to the job.

9. Our tour was more informative because of (her   she) recalling details from the guidebook.

10. When my alarm clock goes off in the morning, (its   it) buzzing always startles me.

11. The instructor congratulated (us   our) finding the correct answer on our own.

Write if each italicized word is a *gerund*, a *participial adjective*, or part of a *verb phrase*.

12. *Playing* his new video game, Joseph waited patiently for his mother. _____

13. *Playing* volleyball regularly can improve eye-hand coordination. _____

14. My brother was *playing* an original song on his electric guitar. _____

15. I was *reaching* into my desk for my math notebook. _____

16. The fans cheered the boys *reaching* the finish line. _____

17. The crowd cheered the boy's *reaching* the finish line. _____

Rewrite each sentence to show the correct use of possessives with gerunds.

18. Michael Phelps swimming at the 2008 Olympics broke numerous records.

_____

19. Frenzied fans all over the world celebrated him winning eight gold medals.

_____

For additional help, review pages 92–93 in your textbook or visit www.voyagesinenglish.com.

Section 5 • 63

5.6 Infinitives as Subjects and Subject Complements

An **infinitive,** when used as a noun, can function as a subject or subject complement. An infinitive can appear alone or in phrases. An **infinitive phrase** consists of the infinitive, its object, and any modifiers.

Underline the infinitive phrase in each sentence. Circle the infinitive in each phrase. Then write *S* (subject) or *SC* (subject complement) to identify how the infinitive phrase is used.

1. An incredible act of kindness is to adopt a stray animal.   _____

2. Our dream is to explore all the countries of Africa.   _____

3. To have a working knowledge of computers is essential.   _____

4. For example, to type on a typewriter is basically obsolete.   _____

5. To go to college is a must in my family.   _____

6. My plan is to attend one of the Ivy League universities.   _____

7. To learn a new language is a challenge and a reward.   _____

8. My idea was to offer more tutoring programs after school.   _____

9. Mina's greatest achievement was to complete her Ph.D.   _____

Complete each sentence with an infinitive or infinitive phrase. Write *subject* or *subject complement* to identify what you added.

10. Something I would like to achieve is _____

_____ . _____

11. _____

is one of my family's traditions.   _____

12. When I reach high school, my plan is _____

_____ . _____

13. _____

is an interesting experiment.   _____

14. _____

is an important rule for me.   _____

15. The purpose of attending college is _____

_____ . _____

© Loyola Press. Voyages in English   Grade 8

For additional help, review pages 94–95 in your textbook or visit www.voyagesinenglish.com.

5.7 Infinitives as Objects

An infinitive, when used as a noun, can function as a direct object. The infinitive and its subject form an **infinitive clause.**

Underline the infinitive in each sentence. Then circle the verb of which the infinitive is the direct object.

1. Mr. Hale encouraged us to brainstorm ideas for the club's fund-raiser.

2. Shyla's horse started to gallop at full speed over the rocky pathway.

3. Our kittens decided to escape the rain by hiding under the house.

4. We mean to find old letters and journals in my grandparents' attic.

5. Tom expects to be the first runner across the finish line.

6. Mia wanted to alleviate the sick child's discomfort.

7. How did you manage to finish all that paperwork?

8. My sister needed me to help her with a special birthday dinner.

9. Where did you direct her to place those notebooks and folders?

10. Before dinner, Elena asked Marco to set the table with plates, silverware, and napkins.

11. Packing a large suitcase, Robby prepared to travel across country with his grandparents.

12. After practice he likes to exercise for several hours in the gym.

Underline the infinitive phrase or clause used as a direct object in each sentence. Circle the subject of the infinitive clauses.

13. Originally named Michael Luther King Jr., he chose to change his first name to Martin.

14. After college Martin decided to study theology at Crozer Theological Seminary.

15. King's interests led him to earn a doctorate degree from Boston University.

16. Gandhi's writings inspired Dr. King to protest in peaceful ways.

17. Dr. King organized groups to boycott the bus system in Montgomery, Alabama.

18. The peaceful protest persuaded the government to change unfair segregation laws.

Write a sentence using each infinitive as a direct object.

19. to climb _____

20. to sing _____

21. to be _____

22. to run _____

For additional help, review pages 96–97 in your textbook or visit www.voyagesinenglish.com.

Section 5 • 65

5.8 Infinitives as Appositives

An infinitive that functions as a noun can be used as an appositive. Infinitive appositives can appear in various positions in a sentence—as a subject, a subject complement, a direct object, or an indirect object.

Underline the infinitive phrase used as an appositive in each sentence.

1. For years people debated a dream, to honor women who had served in the armed forces.

2. On November 6, 1986, President Reagan signed legislation, to authorize a women's memorial, that pleased many people.

3. A national competition, to design a memorial, was held by those in charge of the memorials and monuments in Washington, D.C.

4. The winning plan, to incorporate symbolic light and water into the structure, was chosen unanimously by the commissions.

5. The purpose of this plan, to blend in with the scenic surrounding area, included a setting for the building where it was tucked into the sloping hillside.

6. A fountain and reflecting pool, to represent the flow of life and the voices of women, is set in front of the memorial.

Write the letter of the appositive that best completes each sentence. Then circle the noun each appositive explains.

A. to become a professional ice-skater	**E.** to make balloon animals
B. to win the district championship	**F.** to sell everything at 50 percent off
C. to procrastinate constantly	**G.** to give an oral report
D. to interview our grandparents	**H.** to construct a new hospital

7. We all knew it was Megan's ultimate dream, _____.

8. Our carnival booth's activity, _____, delighted all the children.

9. The builders' plan, _____, was stopped by local landowners.

10. Mr. Greer's assignment, _____, helped us learn about history.

11. This tendency that I have, _____, means that I often rush to meet deadlines.

12. Our team's hope, _____, was finally achieved.

13. The final reduction, _____, helped empty the store's shelves.

14. Her biggest fear, _____, was overcome by taking a speech class.

For additional help, review pages 98–99 in your textbook or visit www.voyagesinenglish.com.

5.9 Infinitives as Adjectives

Infinitives and infinitive phrases can be used as adjectives to describe nouns and pronouns. The infinitive follows the word it modifies.

Underline the infinitive phrase used as an adjective in each sentence. Then write the noun or pronoun the infinitive phrase describes.

1. The street to take to the mall passes near our school.   _____

2. John's attempt to build a doghouse failed miserably.   _____

3. Myra realized she didn't have time to complete her essay.   _____

4. The player to watch in this game is the quarterback.   _____

5. The kitten to adopt is the striped one in that wicker basket.   _____

6. As I checked the cast list, I wanted the lead actor to be me.   _____

7. The horse to ride in the parade is that beautiful chestnut.   _____

8. This health manual outlines a myriad of ways to exercise.   _____

9. I purchased a ticket to ride the roller coaster at the ticket booth.   _____

10. He is always the one to bring delicious, homemade desserts.   _____

11. The instructions to assemble the model car were in three languages.   _____

12. Acceptable guests to invite to the classroom are listed on the board.   _____

Write an infinitive phrase used as an adjective to complete each sentence. Circle the noun the infinitive phrase describes.

13. In South Dakota a great place _____ is Custer State Park.

14. There are numerous activities _____ throughout the park.

15. When visiting Harney Peak, many make the choice _____.

16. Among the hills and prairies, I enjoy long hikes _____.

17. The recreation area provides trails _____.

18. Our plan _____ meant we needed sunscreen.

Write a sentence that uses each infinitive in a phrase that functions as an adjective.

19. to navigate _____

20. to discover _____

21. to be _____

© Loyola Press. Voyages in English   Grade 8

For additional help, review pages 100–101 in your textbook or visit www.voyagesinenglish.com.

5.10 Infinitives as Adverbs

An infinitive or infinitive phrase can be used as an adverb to describe a verb, an adjective, or an adverb. These infinitives follow the words they modify.

Underline the infinitive phrase used as an adverb in each sentence. The word the adverb phrase describes is italicized.

1. Patricia *strolled* to the art fair to view the work of local artists.

2. The obvious creativity of those artists was *exciting* to observe.

3. Some artists *had used* recycled items to construct beautiful sculptures.

4. One artist displayed moving sculptures that were too *tall* to fit in the booth.

5. The judges were looking at the paintings long *enough* to choose the winning artwork.

6. They moved *slowly* from booth to booth to have time for the inspection of unusual pieces.

7. Artists who utilize this fair are *motivated* to sell as many of their artworks as possible.

8. Various carts and wagons *are used* to transport their art at the end of the day.

9. After the booths were removed, the cleaning crew *arrived* to sweep up the remaining litter.

Underline five infinitive phrases used as adverbs in the paragraph. Draw an arrow from each phrase to the verb, adjective, or adverb it describes. Identify the word by writing *V* (verb), *ADJ* (adjective), or *ADV* (adverb) above it.

Recently I went to Washington, D.C., to visit our nation's capital.

I was thrilled to see many original documents written by past

presidents. I visited the Capitol to learn more about our country's

government. I felt extremely patriotic as I walked the grand hallways.

I also visited the White House and was excited to see the place

where our president and his family live. At the Lincoln Memorial, I

admired the statue of my favorite president. I found that I was not in

Washington long enough to see everything on my sightseeing list, but

I had a great time anyway.

For additional help, review pages 102–103 in your textbook or visit www.voyagesinenglish.com.

5.11 Hidden and Split Infinitives

Hidden infinitives appear in sentences without the word *to*. An adverb placed between *to* and the verb results in a **split infinitive.**

Underline the hidden infinitive in each sentence and circle the word that helped you find it.

1. She would prefer to read than participate in sports.
2. Santiago heard the wind whip violently through the treetops.
3. We need not use your truck for our camping trip this weekend.
4. We could see the dancers float about the stage like clouds.
5. Can you help me move into my new apartment tomorrow?
6. Our dog does not dare enter the house when his paws are muddy.
7. Dad made the neighborhood children clean the yard after their games.
8. Stella does nothing but talk on the phone with her boyfriend.
9. I felt the soft breeze from the ocean blow across my face.
10. Mr. Greenberg let me read his copy of the novel since mine is missing.
11. Everyone did little but complain about the amount of work we had to complete.

Rewrite each sentence to eliminate the split infinitive.

12. Ms. Cardoza asked me to completely redesign my science project.

_____

13. My brother asked us to not enter his room without knocking.

_____

14. We asked Mom to quickly show us our list of chores.

_____

15. He stubbornly decided to not cooperate with the rest of the team.

_____

16. Our teacher was unable to immediately locate the answer sheet after the quiz.

_____

17. The chef attempted to slowly pour the hot broth into the ceramic bowl.

_____

For additional help, review pages 104–105 in your textbook or visit www.voyagesinenglish.com.

Section 5 • 69

5.11 Hidden and Split Infinitives

Hidden infinitives appear in sentences without the word *to*. An adverb placed between *to* and the verb results in a **split infinitive.**

Underline the hidden infinitive or the split infinitive in each sentence. Write whether each is a hidden infinitive (*HI*) or a split infinitive (*SI*).

1. A new space project was sent to amazingly orbit Earth in 1998. _____

2. This launch allowed Russia to formally begin construction of a space home. _____

3. Americans delivered more supplies that helped complete the construction. _____

4. These two countries helped build this single, shared structure, the International Space Station. _____

5. After two years of work, astronauts and cosmonauts began to finally move into the International Space Station. _____

6. In 2008 the world watched the project celebrate its 10th birthday. _____

7. The International Space Station had nine rooms to comfortably provide areas for eating, sleeping, and completing experiments. _____

8. Nearly 170 people, representing 15 countries, traveled into space to bravely live and work in the International Space Station. _____

9. Scientists watched astronauts conduct a variety of experiments in space. _____

10. The International Space Station exists today because people dared dream of living in space. _____

11. The knowledge acquired through this endeavor will help improve space travel and exploration for the future. _____

Write a sentence to correct the use of each split infinitive.

12. to finally fly _____

_____

13. to certainly explore _____

_____

14. to secretly discover _____

_____

15. to truly understand _____

_____

© Loyola Press. Voyages in English   Grade 8

For additional help, review pages 104–105 in your textbook or visit www.voyagesinenglish.com.

SECTION 6   Daily Maintenance

6.1 **Reviewing the test, Mrs. Matthews explained the final problem.**
1. What is the participial in the sentence?   _____
2. Is the participial present or past?   _____
3. Is the participial active or passive?   _____
4. What is the participial phrase?   _____
5. Diagram the sentence on another sheet of paper.

6.2 **Winning an art scholarship is Gabriel's goal.**
1. What is the gerund phrase in the sentence?   _____
2. What is its function in the sentence?   _____
3. What is the gerund's direct object?   _____
4. How is the word *goal* used in the sentence?   _____
5. Diagram the sentence on another sheet of paper.

6.3 **My weekend job, walking my neighbors' dogs, is fun.**
1. What is the gerund phrase?   _____
2. What is its function in the sentence?   _____
3. Which word does the gerund rename?   _____
4. Is the possessive noun singular or plural?   _____
5. Diagram the sentence on another sheet of paper.

6.4 **Brad's task for the group project is to create a poster.**

1. What is the infinitive phrase?   _____

2. What is its function in the sentence?   _____

3. Is the infinitive phrase active or passive?   _____

4. What is the adjective phrase?   _____

5. Diagram the sentence on another sheet of paper.

6.5 **At the zoo the children were excited to see the penguins.**

1. What is the infinitive phrase?   _____

2. Is it used as an adjective or an adverb?   _____

3. Which word does the infinitive phrase describe? _____

4. Which noun is an irregular plural?   _____

5. Diagram the sentence on another sheet of paper.

6.1 Types of Adverbs

An **adverb** is a word used to describe a verb, an adjective, or another adverb. It can be an adverb of time, place, manner, degree, affirmation, or negation.

Circle the adverb in each sentence. Then write *time, place, manner, degree, affirmation,* or *negation* to identify the adverb's type.

1. Bailey would never catch the slippery football. _____
2. Handle those valuable ceramics carefully. _____
3. We frequently spend time at the beach. _____
4. Cara searched frantically for her misplaced backpack. _____
5. The spotlight from the approaching helicopter is quite bright. _____
6. The elephants trumpeted loudly as they stampeded. _____
7. Molly remained there while I practiced my speech. _____
8. The principal's speech was long but extremely entertaining. _____
9. I absolutely knew we'd be late if we took the other route. _____
10. The new student seldom receives a poor grade on a test. _____
11. Our coach certainly did expect the whole team to attend. _____

Underline the adverb or adverbs in each sentence. Circle the word the adverb describes and write whether this word is a *verb,* an *adjective,* or an *adverb.*

12. Many tourists eagerly travel to Mazatlan, Mexico. _____
13. People are amazed by the shockingly white sand on the beaches. _____
14. A local delicacy tourists and native people heartily enjoy is shrimp. _____
15. Visitors very rapidly snap photos of the Plaza Machado. _____
16. Families dine on deliciously fresh seafood at local restaurants. _____
17. Bronze statues unexpectedly line the road that runs along the shore. _____

Write a sentence using each type of adverb. Circle the adverb.

18. an adverb of negation describing *do intend* _____

19. an adverb of manner describing *cheered* _____

© Loyola Press. Voyages in English   Grade 8

For additional help, review pages 110–111 in your textbook or visit www.voyagesinenglish.com.

Section 6 • 73

6.2 Interrogative Adverbs and Adverbial Nouns

Interrogative adverbs are used to express or to query reason, place, time, and method. **Adverbial nouns** are nouns that act as adverbs by describing a verb and are used to express time, distance, measure, value, or direction.

Underline the interrogative adverb or adverbial noun in each sentence. Write *IA* (interrogative adverb) or *AN* (adverbial noun) to identify the word.

1. The Abyssinian cat that belongs to my neighbor weighs 13 pounds. _____
2. Specimens of some rare breeds can cost thousands of dollars. _____
3. Why did you decide to go to that lecture? _____
4. The ambient temperature measured 100 degrees or more. _____
5. Our plane flew east, transporting us from Oregon to New York. _____
6. The solar eclipse could be seen for only a few minutes. _____
7. We drove more than 1,800 miles across country last summer. _____
8. When does your baby brother usually wake up from his nap? _____
9. How can we locate information about extinct species of felines? _____
10. The tour group saved many dollars per person on the airline tickets. _____
11. The newly paved road ran southwest toward the downtown area. _____
12. Where is the study sheet I used to prepare for the science competition? _____

Underline each interrogative adverb and adverbial noun. Write *reason*, *place*, *time*, *method*, *distance*, *measure*, *value*, or *direction* to tell what each expresses.

13. How do scientists determine if an animal represents a new species? _____
14. Why were scientists excited about these unexpected discoveries? _____
15. Experts studying the Mekong Delta waited decades to locate new species. _____
16. The Mekong River flows south and east through Asia. _____
17. As it spreads toward the sea, the delta covers 25,000 square miles. _____

Complete each sentence with an interrogative adverb or an adverbial noun. Use the clues in parentheses.

18. _____ should you feed your pet reptile? (method)
19. That diminutive animal weighs only _____. (measure)
20. An hour might go by before you see an anole move _____. (distance)

For additional help, review pages 112–113 in your textbook or visit www.voyagesinenglish.com.

6.2 Interrogative Adverbs and Adverbial Nouns

Interrogative adverbs are used to express or to query reason, place, time, and method. **Adverbial nouns** are nouns that act as adverbs by describing a verb and are used to express time, distance, measure, value, or direction.

Write an interrogative adverb to complete each sentence. Then write *time, reason, method,* or *place* to tell what each adverb expresses.

1. _____ do you like to go in a car? _____

2. _____ is it important to use seat belts when riding in any vehicle? _____

3. _____ is the brand new model of a car designed and built? _____

4. _____ did the mechanic sell his antique sedan? _____

5. _____ on the Internet can you locate information about hybrid cars? _____

6. _____ did your family purchase that new SUV? _____

7. _____ do you think white is one of the most popular auto colors? _____

8. _____ are most people able to drive a car for the first time? _____

Write an adverbial noun to complete each sentence. Write *time, distance, measure, value,* or *direction* to tell what quality each expresses.

9. To finish the Indianapolis 500, drivers must travel 500 _____. _____

10. Most drivers take almost three _____ to complete the race. _____

11. The official display trophy weighs 150 _____. _____

12. A take-home replica trophy measures only 18 _____ high. _____

13. Radio broadcasts of the race are transmitted _____ to Canada. _____

14. During the coldest race ever, temperatures reached only 50 _____. _____

15. Scott Dixon earned over two million _____ in 2008. _____

16. In 1992 Al Unser finished 0.043 _____ before Scott Goodyear. _____

17. The Indianapolis Motor Speedway celebrated 100 _____ of service. _____

Write a sentence with an interrogative adverb or an adverbial noun to express each quality.

18. place _____

19. direction _____

20. value _____

For additional help, review pages 112–113 in your textbook or visit www.voyagesinenglish.com.

Section 6 • 75

6.3 Comparative and Superlative Adverbs

Adverbs can be compared by using the **comparative** and **superlative** forms. Add *more* or *most* before adverbs ending in *ly*, and -*er* or -*est* to adverbs not ending in *ly*. Some adverbs have irregular comparative forms.

Write the correct forms of the adverbs to complete the chart.

	POSITIVE	COMPARATIVE	SUPERLATIVE
1.	slowly		
2.		lower	
3.	happily		
4.		better	
5.	often		
6.			nearest
7.		more/less rigorously	most/least rigorously
8.			most/least actively

Underline the adverb in each sentence. Write *positive*, *comparative*, or *superlative* to identify the form of each adverb.

9. Mount Rainier stands tallest of any peak in the Cascade Range. _____

10. Many climbers successfully ascend Mount Rainier each year. _____

11. Icy conditions increase most dramatically during the winter season. _____

12. The winds blow less severely in summer than in winter. _____

13. Well-prepared climbers most easily reach the summit. _____

14. Mountaineers approach the climb more confidently after training. _____

15. Proper equipment best protects climbers from dangers. _____

16. Mountaineers thoroughly remove their trash after their climb. _____

17. Climber Dee Molenaar artistically portrays Mount Rainier in paintings. _____

18. An 81-year-old man scaled Mount Rainier most determinedly in 1992. _____

Write two sentences about your day so far. Use a comparative adverb in the first sentence and a superlative adverb in the second sentence.

19. _____

20. _____

For additional help, review pages 114–115 in your textbook or visit www.voyagesinenglish.com.

6.4   *As . . . As, So . . . As, and Equally*

> When a comparison is positive, only *as . . . as* may be used. When it is negative, either *as . . . as* or *so . . . as* may be used. Never use *as* between *equally* and the adverb or adjective.

Complete each sentence with *as, so,* or *equally*.

1. Today's hike was _____ difficult as yesterday's hike.

2. I can juggle many balls _____ skillfully as the juggler at the fair.

3. This clothing is not _____ expensive as the items on that rack.

4. In this class the dancers are _____ trained for classical ballet.

5. The amateur musicians played _____ skillfully as the professionals.

6. The two students are _____ matched for the mathematics competition.

7. Mount Whitney isn't nearly _____ high as Mount Everest.

8. She can't comprehend the material _____ quickly as the rest of the group.

Write a sentence for each topic that includes *as . . . as, so . . . as,* or *equally*.

9. Your friend tells a funnier joke than you do.

_____

10. The championship game was more exciting last year.

_____

11. The sauce is spicy and so is the spaghetti.

_____

12. Your class did an efficient job collecting cans for a food drive both this year and last year.

_____

13. It took less than an hour to finish your homework on Monday and Tuesday.

_____

14. The new computer downloads information more quickly than the old one.

_____

15. Two team jerseys were inexpensive because of a sale.

_____

For additional help, review pages 116–117 in your textbook or visit www.voyagesinenglish.com.

Section 6 • 77

6.4 As . . . As, So . . . As, and *Equally*

When a comparison is positive, only *as . . . as* is used. When it is negative, either *as . . . as* or *so . . . as* is used. Never use *as* between *equally* and the adverb or adjective.

Circle the word that correctly completes each sentence. Write *positive*, *negative*, or *equal* to identify each choice.

1. I do not reside (equally   so) near Lake Michigan as my cousin.   _____

2. Swimming and boating on the lake are (equally   equally as) popular.   _____

3. Working is not (equally   so) enjoyable as a day on the beach.   _____

4. The lake's history is (as   equally as) intriguing as a complex puzzle.   _____

5. Volcanoes affected the lake's formation (as   so) much as glaciers did.   _____

6. Today, it isn't (equally   so) large as when it was first formed.   _____

7. The lake was (as   so) needed for fur trading as for moving goods.   _____

8. Many people were (equally   so) dependent on the lake for fish.   _____

9. Each of the Great Lakes is (equally   as) important in many ways.   _____

10. Their proximity is (as   so) important to the United States as to Canada.   _____

11. The lakes' outline is (as   so) recognizable as the shape of your hand.   _____

Write sentences using *as . . . as, as . . . so*, or *equally* to show comparisons for these situations.

12. Positively compare two kinds of pets.

_____

13. Compare two equal weather events.

_____

14. Negatively compare two vehicles.

_____

15. Positively compare beach activities.

_____

16. Negatively compare two fund-raisers.

_____

For additional help, review pages 116–117 in your textbook or visit www.voyagesinenglish.com.

6.5 Adverb Phrases and Clauses

An **adverb phrase** is a prepositional phrase used as an adverb telling *when, where, why,* and *how.* An **adverb clause,** a dependent clause that acts as an adverb, tells *how, when, where, why, to what extent,* or *under what condition.*

Underline the adverb phrases. Circle the word or words each phrase describes.

1. Last week my family rode on the Agawa Canyon Tour Train.

2. We boarded this long train early in the morning.

3. We admired the scenery as we traveled through Canada's Agawa Canyon.

4. The window view is not cluttered with road signs or traffic lights.

5. All the train's passengers were mesmerized by the bright hues.

6. The trees were covered with red, yellow, orange, and gold leaves.

7. The train also carried us high above sparkling rivers and deep canyons.

8. Throughout the trip we learned entertaining details from our tour guide.

9. Finally, this train rumbled between steep rock walls to the canyon bottom.

10. We disembarked from the tourist train for two hours so we could explore the canyon.

11. We eagerly hiked along winding rocky trails beside massive thundering waterfalls.

12. On the return trip to Sault Ste. Marie, I ate lunch in the dining car with my sister.

Underline the adverb clauses. Circle the word or words each clause describes.

13. Because we enjoy hiking, my aunt and I purchased sturdy boots.

14. Although it can be confusing, I read many articles about the selection of hiking boots.

15. After we located the store, we studied the footwear in the display window.

16. My aunt and I planned our next adventure as we shopped for boots.

17. Since trails are often wet, I considered several waterproof styles of boots.

18. I prefer lightweight footwear until the temperature falls below 30 degrees.

19. My uncle wears steel-reinforced boots when he sets out on a five-day trek.

20. If I expect to carry a heavy backpack, I will require boots that support my ankles.

21. Today I tested six pairs of hiking boots before I selected a pair with a rubber sole.

22. When the boots fit properly, I avoid blisters and irritations on my sensitive feet.

23. New boots should be worn during normal walking activities until they are broken in.

24. While my aunt purchased our new footwear, I studied the dance shoes in the window.

For additional help, review pages 118–119 in your textbook or visit www.voyagesinenglish.com.

6.5   Adverb Phrases and Clauses

> An **adverb phrase** is a prepositional phrase used as an adverb telling *when, where, why,* and *how.* An **adverb clause,** a dependent clause that acts as an adverb, tells *how, when, where, why, to what extent,* or *under what condition.*

Underline the adverb phrases and clauses. Circle the word each phrase or clause describes. Write *phrase* or *clause* to identify each one.

1. Last summer my family traveled to Italy.   _____

2. Since we had one week, we planned to visit three cities.   _____

3. After we considered many cities, we chose Venice.   _____

4. We rode a gondola and cruised through the canals.   _____

5. Then we visited St. Mark's Square and gazed in wonder.   _____

6. My family and I walked until our feet were aching.   _____

7. After we rested at our hotel, we visited Florence.   _____

8. I could see, as we traveled through the city, lovely Florentine art. _____

9. When I saw the statues, I realized what masterpieces they were.   _____

10. Later we flew in a small airplane to the fascinating city of Rome. _____

11. We arrived at the Rome Fiumicino Airport late in the evening.   _____

12. We immediately went to the Trevi Fountain before we forgot.   _____

13. I tossed a coin into the water as I made a wish.   _____

14. We rented bikes before we headed into the countryside.   _____

15. All of us were overwhelmed by amazing memories of Italy.   _____

16. We felt exhausted because the flight home was so long.   _____

Revise each sentence by adding both an adverb phrase and an adverb clause.

17. I traveled.

_____

18. My cousins drive.

_____

19. The tourists explored.

_____

© Loyola Press. Voyages in English   Grade 8

For additional help, review pages 118–119 in your textbook or visit www.voyagesinenglish.com.

SECTION 7 Daily Maintenance

7.1 **The cheering fans rushed quickly to the concert stage.**
1. Which word is a participial adjective?   _____
2. Which word is an adverb?   _____
3. Is it an adverb of time, manner, or place?   _____
4. What is the adverb phrase?   _____
5. Diagram the sentence on another sheet of paper.

7.2 **Brett's new hobby, restoring model trains, is very difficult.**
1. What is the gerund phrase in the sentence?   _____
2. What is its function in the sentence?   _____
3. Which word is an adverb?   _____
4. What part of speech is the word it describes?   _____
5. Diagram the sentence on another sheet of paper.

7.3 **Why did you decide to take the babysitting job?**
1. What is the infinitive phrase?   _____
2. What is its function in the sentence?   _____
3. Which word is an interrogative adverb?   _____
4. Which word is a participial adjective?   _____
5. Diagram the sentence on another sheet of paper.

7.4 **My friend Jerrod dances less awkwardly than I.**
1. What is the adverb in the sentence? _____
2. Is the adverb's form comparative or superlative? _____
3. How is the word *Jerrod* used in the sentence? _____
4. What is the person and number of the pronoun? _____
5. Diagram the sentence on another sheet of paper.

7.5 **Janet works best after she takes a short nap.**
1. Which are the verbs in the sentence? _____
2. What is the adverb? _____
3. Is the adverb's form comparative or superlative? _____
4. What is the adverb clause? _____
5. Diagram the sentence on another sheet of paper.

7.6 **When Daisy returned from France, she showed me her photographs.**
1. What is the adverb clause in the sentence? _____
2. Which word does it describe? _____
3. What is the direct object? _____
4. What part of speech is the indirect object? _____
5. Diagram the sentence on another sheet of paper.

7.1 Single and Multiword Prepositions

A **preposition** shows the relationship between a noun or pronoun and another word in the sentence. **Multiword prepositions** are made up of more than one word but are treated as single words.

Circle the two prepositions in each sentence.

1. The juice from the grapes on the vine tasted sweet.

2. The zookeeper arrived with food for the giant turtles.

3. We placed all the grain into the barrel behind the barn.

4. I viewed hundreds of stars through my new telescope.

5. We strolled beyond the wooden fence to the playground.

6. Kathleen wrote her name in the box and placed a stamp above her name.

7. The park near my house features free concerts during the summer.

8. The blaring sound from the TV was too distracting for me.

Circle the multiword preposition in each sentence.

9. In spite of the heat, we spent the day at the beach.

10. On account of the cloudy skies, I couldn't observe Saturn.

11. Because of the heavy snowfall, school closed for the day.

12. Please carefully back the minivan out of the garage for me.

13. The grocer positioned the sale sign in front of the red grapes.

14. I decided to concentrate on rain forest insects instead of snakes in my report.

15. In addition to the pickles, we preserved many other vegetables from our farm.

Complete each sentence with a preposition: *according to, toward, after, in spite of, between, beside, in addition to,* **or** *during.*

16. The baseball game continued _____ the pouring rain.

17. The kittens slept _____ the mother cat and the fireplace.

18. We enjoyed a delicious dinner _____ seeing the movie.

19. _____ my oral presentation, the class listened attentively.

20. The plane began its slow ascent _____ the cloud-filled sky.

21. _____ newspaper reports, the massive hurricane struck at 2:30 a.m.

22. The audience applauded loudly for the band _____ the performance.

For additional help, review pages 124–125 in your textbook or visit www.voyagesinenglish.com.

Section 7 • 83

7.2 Troublesome Prepositions

Certain groups of **troublesome prepositions** are often confused. To use them correctly, you should understand the differences among them.

Circle the preposition that correctly completes each sentence.

1. Sean is angry (at   with) the idea of arriving late again.
2. Carlos differs (with   on) Mom over the college he will attend.
3. He ran (like   as if) he had a band of ravenous wolves after him.
4. Taylor was angry (with   at) Elijah for forgetting her birthday.
5. We differ (with   on) the types of attire and accessories we choose to wear.
6. This automobile differs (with   from) that older vehicle in size and speed.
7. How did you decide (between   among) sandals and walking shoes?
8. Her new kitten attempts to stalk prey (like   as if) a full-grown tiger.
9. We will choose (between   among) five students for class president.
10. Please place the completed diagram (besides   beside) your science experiment.

Complete each sentence with a preposition from the box.

beside	besides	in	into	between	among	differ with
differ on	differ from	like	as if	as though	angry with	angry at

11. A florist works _____ many varieties of flowers.
12. Some florists prepare flowers _____ large warehouses.
13. Others decide _____ mall shops and small booths on the street.
14. _____ selecting blooms to sell, each florist arranges the flowers decoratively.
15. Some florists design bouquets _____ the flowers are for their own family.
16. I could not be _____ a friend who brought me a sweet bouquet from a florist.

Write a sentence using each preposition: *differ with*, *differ on*, and *differ from*.

17. _____
18. _____
19. _____

© Loyola Press. Voyages in English   Grade 8

For additional help, review pages 126–127 in your textbook or visit www.voyagesinenglish.com.

7.3 Words Used as Adverbs and Prepositions

Some words can be either adverbs or prepositions. A preposition is always part of a phrase ending with a noun or a pronoun as its object.

Write *preposition* or *adverb* to identify each italicized word.

1. Above us the soaring jets streaked *across* the sky.   _____

2. The explosive noise quickly caused us to glance *up*.   _____

3. How many jets swept *over* the throngs of people?   _____

4. The crowd cheered appreciatively when a jet rolled *over*.   _____

5. We moved *toward* the fence to secure a better view.   _____

6. Suddenly, I heard a loud boom as another jet flew *past*.   _____

7. That powerful jet must have streaked directly *above*.   _____

8. A loud cheer erupted *from* the people in the crowd.   _____

9. After the show, we all went *inside* to share refreshments.   _____

Complete each sentence with *behind, beside, by, down, downward, in, near, off, on, outside,* or *under*. Write whether each is an adverb (*A*) or a preposition (*P*).

10. We are visiting the giant water park _____ my home.   _____

11. First, I splash and jump _____ the huge wave pool.   _____

12. Next, we push _____ from the top of the tallest water slide.   _____

13. We rapidly slide _____ until we crash into the pool.   _____

14. The family tube ride gradually spiralled _____ through a tunnel.   _____

15. We even glided _____ a gushing waterfall, which soaked all of us.   _____

16. Then we all relaxed and ate our scrumptious picnic lunch _____.   _____

17. Finally, I floated _____ my brother _____ the lazy river.   _____

Write a sentence using each word as an adverb or a preposition.

18. away _____

19. beyond _____

20. inside _____

21. beneath _____

For additional help, review pages 128–129 in your textbook or visit www.voyagesinenglish.com.

Section 7 • 85

7.4 Prepositional Phrases as Adjectives

An **adjective phrase** is a prepositional phrase that describes a noun or pronoun.

Underline the adjective phrase in each sentence. Then circle the noun or pronoun the adjective phrase describes.

1. Our oceans contain almost countless species of sharks.

2. The eyes of most sharks are extremely sensitive.

3. The great white shark is one of the best-known species.

4. These sharks live in the temperate waters of many oceans.

5. The actual lifespan for this shark can reach 100 years.

6. Some publications about sharks have frightened people.

7. In fact, most sharks don't desire interaction with people.

8. A shark has many tiny holes on its head that help it find prey.

9. These holes, ampullae of Lorenzini, help sharks detect electric fields.

10. Sharks first appeared eons before the time that today's fish first existed.

11. The time before the age of dinosaurs is when sharks first developed.

12. The numerous teeth in a shark's mouth are razor-sharp and tilted inward.

13. Great white sharks grow new rows of teeth every one to two weeks.

14. Extinction of the giant megalodon shark occurred nearly 1.6 million years ago.

15. In general the males of each species are significantly smaller than the females.

16. The waters off Costa Rica is a place where many species congregate by the hundreds.

Rewrite each sentence, replacing the italicized words with an adjective phrase.

17. The Farallon Islands, a *wildlife refuge*, is a popular shark feeding ground.

_____

18. In 1992 white sharks were added to the *protected species list* in California.

_____

19. These amazing sharks swim many times faster than the best *Olympic swimmer*.

_____

For additional help, review pages 130–131 in your textbook or visit www.voyagesinenglish.com.

7.5 Prepositional Phrases as Adverbs

Adverb phrases are prepositional phrases used as adverbs to describe verbs, adjectives, or other adverbs. They answer the questions *how, when, where, why, to what extent,* and *under what condition.*

Underline the adverb phrase in each sentence. Circle the word or words the adverb phrase describes.

1. During the Middle Ages many boys yearned to become knights.

2. You may wonder about a boy's path to knighthood.

3. Usually, a boy started as a page, an assistant to a knight.

4. An eager young page displayed extreme loyalty to his knight.

5. A page was required to learn courtly manners early in his training.

6. Before a hunt, the page prepared the falcons and hawks.

7. In addition to the preparations, a page practiced hunting skills.

8. At the youthful age of 14, the page proudly became a squire.

9. Squires assisted knights with their horses, spurs, and weapons.

10. During this training a squire worked exhaustingly hard every day.

11. After seven years a successful squire was usually knighted.

12. To confer knighthood, a nobleman dubbed a squire on the shoulders, using a sword.

13. The new knight would always perform with bravery and honesty.

14. An honorable and noble knight served his king with loyalty for life.

Rewrite each sentence using two adverb phrases that describe the italicized word.

15. I *volunteer.*

   _____

16. Volunteers are *helpful.*

   _____

17. This volunteer arrived *early.*

   _____

18. Some volunteers *work.*

   _____

For additional help, review pages 132–133 in your textbook
or visit www.voyagesinenglish.com.

7.6   Prepositional Phrases as Nouns

A prepositional phrase can be used as a noun in any position where a noun can be used in a sentence. A prepositional phrase can act as a subject or a subject complement.

Underline each prepositional phrase used as a noun. Write *S* if the phrase functions as a subject. Write *SC* if the phrase functions as a subject complement.

1. Beside that meadow was where we noticed the herd of deer. _____

2. A fantastic day to visit a community park is on a national holiday. _____

3. Under the tree is my favorite place to read a novel. _____

4. After dinner was a wonderful time to enjoy a long walk. _____

5. Toward the beach is the direction we should head next. _____

6. My favorite location to nap will be among those wildflowers. _____

7. A risky time to talk on the phone is during a lightning storm. _____

8. Because of the snow was the reason we had to cancel the play. _____

9. One very unusual place to pitch a tent is in the vegetable garden. _____

10. The spot where we will make our campsite should be over this mountain. _____

11. At the head of that trail is the location where we spotted the black bear. _____

Complete each sentence by writing a prepositional noun phrase.

12. _____ is where she put the dirty dishes.

13. The area to repair the bicycle is _____.

14. _____ is my favorite time of day.

15. The reason we rode our bikes was _____.

16. _____ is the best place to see tennis.

17. My normal time for watching TV is _____.

18. _____ was my favorite place to relax.

19. My favorite time to eat pizza is _____.

20. _____ is where we spotted the squirrel.

21. _____ was where my wheelchair rolled.

22. The answers to the test questions will be _____.

23. _____ will be the likely solution.

© Loyola Press. Voyages in English   Grade 8

For additional help, review pages 134–135 in your textbook or visit www.voyagesinenglish.com.

7.6 Prepositional Phrases as Nouns

A prepositional phrase can be used as a noun in any position where a noun can be used in a sentence. A prepositional phrase can act as a subject or a subject complement.

Underline the prepositional phrase in each sentence. Write whether each phrase is an adjective (*ADJ*) phrase, an adverb (*ADV*) phrase, or a noun (*N*) phrase.

1. In front of an audience is where the fashion model first appears. _____
2. The fashion models gracefully saunter down a long catwalk. _____
3. Another job possibility can be modeling for magazine or billboard ads. _____
4. Commercials on television also provide challenging modeling jobs. _____
5. In toy store sale catalogs would be one place requiring child models. _____
6. With a comp, or photo, card is the professional way to audition. _____
7. A professional model must work cooperatively with photographers. _____
8. Healthy hair, skin, and teeth are important in the modeling profession. _____
9. The graceful hands of a model may advertise elegant jewelry. _____
10. By means of Internet research is an effective process to locate agents. _____
11. Reference books about fashion and print modeling are helpful resources. _____
12. At professional modeling agencies are resources to acquire information. _____
13. On modeling jobs are opportunities to meet directors and magazine editors. _____
14. Youth models need special work permits from the school district. _____

Write a sentence that uses each prepositional phrase as a noun.

15. on a stage

_____

16. in the talent show

_____

17. before a rehearsal

_____

18. during the audition

_____

SECTION 8 | Daily Maintenance

8.1 The jewelry in this display case was made by my sister.
1. What are the prepositions in the sentence?   _____
2. What is the adjective phrase?   _____
3. What is the adverb phrase?   _____
4. Which word does the adverb phrase describe?   _____
5. Diagram the sentence on another sheet of paper.

8.2 Because of his hard work, Rick received a bonus for the month of June.
1. What is the multiword preposition?   _____
2. Which prepositional phrase describes *received*?   _____
3. What are the single-word prepositions?   _____
4. Which prepositional phrase describes *month*?   _____
5. Diagram the sentence on another sheet of paper.

8.3 Taj and Maya slowly walked under the swaying trees.
1. Is the subject or the predicate compound?   _____
2. Is *slowly* an adverb of degree or manner?   _____
3. Is *under* used as an adverb or a preposition?   _____
4. Which word is a participial adjective?   _____
5. Diagram the sentence on another sheet of paper.

8.4 The author of this play also wrote a novel about the Civil War.
1. What are the prepositions in the sentence?   _____
2. Which prepositional phrase describes *author*?   _____
3. Which prepositional phrase describes *novel*?   _____
4. What part of speech is the word *also*?   _____
5. Diagram the sentence on another sheet of paper.

8.5 **The goal of the meeting is to plan the club's party.**
1. What is the simple subject in the sentence? _____
2. What is the infinitive phrase? _____
3. Is it used as a subject or a subject complement? _____
4. What is the adjective phrase? _____
5. Diagram the sentence on another sheet of paper.

8.6 **Many of my friends have seen this movie already.**
1. What is the adjective phrase in the sentence? _____
2. Does this phrase describe a noun or pronoun? _____
3. What is the tense of the verb? _____
4. Is *already* used as a preposition or an adverb? _____
5. Diagram the sentence on another sheet of paper.

8.7 **We landed at the airport early in the morning.**
1. How is *at the airport* used in the sentence? _____
2. Which word does it describe? _____
3. Is *early* used as an adjective or an adverb? _____
4. How is *in the morning* used in the sentence? _____
5. Diagram the sentence on another sheet of paper.

8.8 **The hiking trail on the left is perfect for experienced hikers.**
1. Which phrase is used as an adverb? _____
2. Which word does it describe? _____
3. Which prepositional phrase describes *trail*? _____
4. Is *perfect* the subject or subject complement? _____
5. Diagram the sentence on another sheet of paper.

8.9 **My favorite activity is collecting vintage baseball cards.**
1. What is the complete subject in the sentence?   _____
2. What is the gerund phrase?   _____
3. Which word is the gerund?   _____
4. Which word is the object of the gerund?   _____
5. Diagram the sentence on another sheet of paper.

8.10 **Abby will type the research report while Nolan makes several posters.**
1. What is the adverb clause in the sentence?   _____
2. Which word is a subordinate conjunction?   _____
3. Which words are modified by the adverb clause?   _____
4. What type of adjective is the word *several*?   _____
5. Diagram the sentence on another sheet of paper.

8.11 **Under a shady tree is the perfect spot for a picnic.**
1. What is the subject complement in the sentence?   _____
2. What kind of phrase is *Under a shady tree*?   _____
3. How is it used in the sentence?   _____
4. What is the adjective phrase?   _____
5. Diagram the sentence on another sheet of paper.

8.1 Kinds of Sentences

A **sentence** is a group of words that expresses a complete thought. The essential parts of a sentence are the **subject** and the **predicate.** Sentences can be **declarative, interrogative, imperative,** or **exclamatory.**

Write *declarative, interrogative, imperative,* or *exclamatory* to identify each sentence. Then write the correct end punctuation.

1. That was such an incredible football game _____

2. Come with me to play volleyball this afternoon _____

3. Please help complete all the chores this weekend _____

4. My best friend gave me a watch for my birthday _____

5. Did Andrea remember to walk the dog after class _____

6. The grainy sand felt warm and smooth between my toes _____

7. Is Noah the most talented tennis player on the varsity team _____

8. What an amazing adventure you had in Rome _____

Draw a line between the complete subject and complete predicate in each sentence. Then underline the simple subject and circle the simple predicate.

9. Trained horses jump fences as part of a competition.

10. Our active puppy can catch spinning discs in the air.

11. My friend's Persian cat fetches pom-poms on command.

12. Many breeds of animals are trained to perform exciting stunts.

13. Brandon's talented dog demonstrates a variety of amusing tricks.

14. The amazing dolphin might be one of the most intelligent animals on earth.

15. Trainers will demonstrate the different techniques for working with animals.

16. Many spectators watch killer whales and dolphins in amusement park shows.

Write a declarative, an imperative, an exclamatory, and an interrogative sentence. In each sentence, underline the simple subject and circle the simple predicate.

17. _____

18. _____

19. _____

20. _____

For additional help, review pages 140–141 in your textbook or visit www.voyagesinenglish.com.

8.2 Adjective and Adverb Phrases

A **prepositional phrase** includes a preposition, the object of the preposition, and modifiers. A **participial phrase** contains a present or past participle and related words. **Infinitive phrases** include an infinitive and any related words.

Write whether each italicized phrase is *prepositional*, *participial*, or *infinitive*.

1. A shelter is a good place *to bring kittens and puppies*. _____

2. Each animal there is treated *with outstanding love and care*. _____

3. Every creature eventually is settled *in a suitable home*. _____

4. Veterinarians volunteer *to treat sick and injured animals*. _____

5. Numerous people donate their time *to help the shelter staff*. _____

6. Many animals *in the shelter* need immediate medical care. _____

7. There is never enough money *to pay for necessary services*. _____

8. *Providing comfort to animals*, people donate blankets, food, and toys. _____

9. Youth organizations, *selling crafts or baked goods*, raise needed funds. _____

Underline the adjective or adverb phrase in each sentence. Write *ADJ* (adjective phrase) or *ADV* (adverb phrase) to identify each phrase.

10. These signs are part of a special pet adoption program. _____

11. The special pet adoption program began during the summer. _____

12. Many people can volunteer to walk and feed the shelter animals. _____

13. The shelter staff work diligently to find the animals new homes. _____

14. Adoption information is often available at fairs and exhibitions. _____

15. A key part of the program is free spaying and neutering. _____

16. Gaining local popularity, the shelter receives many donations. _____

17. Expanding its services, the shelter recently began taking reptiles. _____

18. The shelter provides reptile cages with heat lamps and water bowls. _____

Write a sentence using each adjective or adverb phrase.

19. to rescue stray dogs _____

20. for their new pet _____

21. coordinating all services _____

22. using a leather leash _____

© Loyola Press. Voyages in English   Grade 8

For additional help, review pages 142–143 in your textbook or visit www.voyagesinenglish.com.

8.3 Adjective Clauses

An **adjective clause,** one type of dependent clause, describes a noun or pronoun. Most adjective clauses begin with a **relative pronoun.** Some adjective clauses begin with a **subordinate conjunction.**

Underline the adjective clause in each sentence. Circle the relative pronoun or subordinate conjunction.

1. The automobile that my aunt drove was candy-apple red.

2. Summer is the season when my family travels to the beach.

3. This is the proud coach whose team won the playoff game.

4. Tyler was the student whom we chose for class president.

5. Michael showed us the restaurant where he is employed as a chef.

6. January is the month when we celebrate five birthdays in my family.

7. Science, which is my strongest subject, is difficult for some students.

8. Ms. Gomez told us about the entrance exams that we'll complete soon.

9. Maya visited the racetrack stables where her beloved horse is boarded.

10. My broken leg was the reason why I did not attend the ski trip last week.

11. His grandmother was the one who taught him to prepare many gourmet foods.

Write an adjective clause to complete each sentence. Circle the noun each clause describes.

12. The large mountain, _____, was difficult to climb.

13. California and Hawaii are two places _____.

14. India's tigers, _____, are in danger of extinction.

15. The Iditarod is a daring race _____.

16. A view of our unique capitol building is a reason _____.

Rewrite each sentence, adding an adjective clause. Circle the noun each adjective clause describes.

17. The children's museum has interactive exhibits.

   _____

18. Hawaii is famous for active volcanoes.

   _____

For additional help, review pages 144–145 in your textbook or visit www.voyagesinenglish.com.

Section 8 • 95

8.4 Restrictive and Nonrestrictive Clauses

An adjective clause that is essential to the meaning of the sentence is a **restrictive clause**. A **nonrestrictive clause** is an adjective clause that is not essential to the meaning of the sentence.

Underline the adjective clause in each sentence. Write _R_ if the clause is restrictive and _NR_ if the clause is nonrestrictive.

1. The gold earrings that I purchased are for my mother. _____

2. Throw away the umbrella that won't open properly. _____

3. Yellow, which is my favorite color, illuminates a room. _____

4. The oranges that you picked yesterday are in that wicker basket. _____

5. The kite that is lodged in our tree is tangled in the branches. _____

6. Devon, who is a talented athlete, made the football team. _____

7. Several restaurants that she suggested sounded interesting. _____

8. Neena, who is new this year, qualified for the tennis team. _____

9. The king who had prevailed in battle was the only one to return home. _____

10. The eggs that dropped on the floor made an enormous mess. _____

Underline the adjective clause in each sentence. Add commas where necessary.

11. Yosemite National Park which is known for its waterfalls offers many water activities.

12. Park visitors who follow safety rules are welcome to swim in the Merced River.

13. Boaters enjoy rafting on the Merced River which has calm and whitewater areas.

14. Some tourists prefer kayaking on Tenaya Lake which is quieter than the river.

15. Fish that are caught in the Toulomne River must be 12 inches or less in length.

Use the information in parentheses to write an adjective clause to complete each sentence.

16. Yosemite, _____, is a favorite vacation spot. (nonrestrictive)

17. A backpack _____ was recommended. (restrictive)

18. Our club, _____, prefers walking tours. (nonrestrictive)

19. The guide book, _____, offered many ideas. (nonrestrictive)

20. The people _____ will be guaranteed a ticket. (restrictive)

For additional help, review pages 146–147 in your textbook or visit www.voyagesinenglish.com.

8.4 Restrictive and Nonrestrictive Clauses

An adjective clause that is essential to the meaning of the sentence is a **restrictive clause.** A **nonrestrictive clause** is an adjective clause that is not essential to the meaning of the sentence.

In each sentence, underline the adjective clause and circle the noun it describes. Write _R_ (restrictive) _or NR_ (nonrestrictive) to identify the type of clause.

1. Missouri offers a brochure that explains how to catch fish.   _____

2. This guidebook, which simplifies fishing skills, encourages novices.   _____

3. Some lakes and rivers are stocked with trout, which attract anglers.   _____

4. Any angler whose permit is valid can fish in Missouri lakes and rivers.   _____

5. Fancy poles and bait, which are sold in sports stores, are not needed.   _____

6. Photos that appear in the guide demonstrate basic casting techniques.   _____

7. The reel, which holds the fishing line, can be open face or closed face.   _____

8. People who are learning to fish can practice casting in a park or yard.   _____

9. A bait chart describes the type of bait that each fish prefers.   _____

10. Jigs, spinners, and plugs are lures that novice fishers might use.   _____

11. Fishers often decide to release the fish that they have caught.   _____

12. Special events, which are free for families, let kids experience fishing.   _____

13. The state of Missouri, which provides the guide, wants fishing to be fun. _____

Rewrite each sentence, adding a restrictive or nonrestrictive clause.

14. This man caught three bluegill fish.

_____

15. He had fished in the rivers of Missouri for many years.

_____

16. Then he shared his bait with me.

_____

17. Fishing is a relaxing hobby in Missouri.

_____

For additional help, review pages 146–147 in your textbook or visit www.voyagesinenglish.com.

8.5 Adverb Clauses

Adverb clauses describe verbs, adjectives, or other adverbs. Adverb clauses tell *where, when, why, in what way, to what extent,* or *under what condition.*

Underline the adverb clause in each sentence. Circle each subordinate conjunction.

1. After the game ended, we quickly drove home.

2. I will serve dinner as soon as the guests arrive.

3. While Derek washed the car, Carla mowed the lawn.

4. Because Jim was embarrassed, his face turned red.

5. I didn't know what to do when I missed the bus to school.

6. The class cheered when Mr. Sanders postponed the test.

7. Those children acted as if they could remain awake all night.

8. We finished our homework before we hurried to the movie.

9. She will make the varsity team if she does well at the tryouts.

10. Although the water was cold, we enjoyed swimming in the river.

11. At the museum we found interesting exhibits wherever we looked.

12. Dad will take us to the park so long as the sun continues to shine.

13. Unless the snowstorm becomes more severe, we will visit our grandparents.

14. The football team held a bake sale so that new uniforms could be purchased.

15. Even though the microphones did not function, the choir continued its performance.

Finish the adverb clause to complete each sentence.

16. Although _____,
    she still felt nervous during her performance.

17. When _____,
    I walked on the beach and went scuba diving.

18. As long as _____,
    we could do our homework in the learning center.

19. Since the delivery van stalled, _____
    _____.

20. You can improve your grades if _____
    _____.

21. Mom sliced the roast while _____
    _____.

© Loyola Press. Voyages in English   Grade 8

For additional help, review pages 148–149 in your textbook or visit www.voyagesinenglish.com.

8.6 Noun Clauses as Subjects

A **noun clause** is a dependent clause used as a noun. A noun clause can function as a subject in a sentence. A noun clause used as a subject generally takes the singular form of the verb.

Underline the noun clause used as the subject in each sentence. Circle the word that introduces each clause.

1. That the five singers were anxious was apparent to everyone.

2. That Tia was the best singer in the competition was not in question.

3. Who would win the contest would be decided by an audience vote.

4. Whatever the audience chose to do affected every contestant's future.

5. That we were so excited about her performance caused Tia to feel confident.

6. Whoever was selected as the winner would earn a music school scholarship.

7. How Tia forgot the lyrics to her song was a shock to competitors and viewers.

8. Whether she recalled the words in time worried Tia as she walked off the stage.

9. When each performer took a final bow signaled the moment for audience voting.

10. Why Tia deserved that music scholarship was obvious to everyone in the theater.

11. That Tia was chosen as the winner was the cause of tremendous excitement and joy.

Write a noun clause used as a subject to complete each sentence.

12. _____

was an amazing accomplishment.

13. _____

was a thrilling moment.

14. _____

may be considered her greatest talent.

15. _____

was noticeable to spectators.

16. _____

has always fascinated me.

17. _____

creates a mood of mystery.

For additional help, review pages 150–151 in your textbook or visit www.voyagesinenglish.com.

Section 8 • 99

8.6   Noun Clauses as Subjects

A **noun clause** is a dependent clause used as a noun. A noun clause can function as a subject in a sentence. A noun clause used as a subject generally takes the singular form of the verb.

Complete each sentence with an introductory word. Then underline the noun clause that is used as a subject.

1. _____ Barack Obama would be sworn in as president was significant.

2. _____ my family could attend the inauguration was a big decision.

3. _____ I learned about my family's plans was an exciting moment for me.

4. _____ more than a million spectators came to Washington, D.C., amazed us.

5. _____ so many came to this inauguration was to witness an historical event.

6. _____ giant screens stood along the Mall allowed us to view the ceremony.

7. _____ occurred that day in January was broadcast around the world.

8. _____ the ceremony took place was the impressive west side of the Capitol.

9. _____ held the Bible as Obama took the presidential oath was his wife.

10. _____ Obama finished his oath was a time of exuberant cheers from the crowd.

11. _____ the U.S. Navy Band played the anthem was a dramatic end.

12. _____ we would observe the new president in the parade was our next concern.

13. _____ watched the parade was impressed by bands from across the country.

Write a sentence that uses each noun clause as the subject.

14. whatever we choose to do

_____

15. what my family saw

_____

16. whether I enjoy the day

_____

17. that being president is a challenging job

_____

© Loyola Press. Voyages in English   **Grade 8**

For additional help, review pages 150–151 in your textbook or visit www.voyagesinenglish.com.

8.7 Noun Clauses as Subject Complements

A noun clause can be used as a subject complement. A linking verb joins the subject to the noun clause used as a subject complement.

Underline the noun clause used as a subject complement in each sentence. Circle the subject about which the noun clause gives more information.

1. The best solution is that everyone brings food to share.

2. Yoga is what my sister studies at the recreation center.

3. Shane's idea is that we take our vacation in New Zealand.

4. My only worry is that you remain out too late without calling.

5. The main problem was that Jack decided to give up painting.

6. The reason remained that Evan wanted to study art in Europe.

7. Mom's favorite vacation was when Dad took her to Venice, Italy.

8. The best activity might be when we all go swimming in the ocean.

9. My favorite hour is when the class heads outside to play softball.

10. The teacher's concern was how teams could be assigned fairly.

11. The most valuable team member is whoever shows the most spirit.

12. The question now was who would take over after Jeffrey departed.

13. The fact remains that Galileo improved a telescope developed by someone else.

Rewrite each sentence to include a noun clause as the subject complement.

14. Galileo was the chosen name for the spacecraft.

   _____

15. Astronaut Shannon Lucid was the one releasing Galileo from the shuttle in 1989.

   _____

16. The goal of the Galileo probe in 1995 was learning about Jupiter's rings.

   _____

17. The scientists' concern was the pictures displaying amazing views of Jupiter.

   _____

© Loyola Press. Voyages in English Grade 8

For additional help, review pages 152–153 in your textbook or visit www.voyagesinenglish.com.

Section 8 • 101

8.7 Noun Clauses as Subject Complements

A noun clause can be used as a subject complement. A linking verb joins the subject to the noun clause used as a subject complement.

Underline the noun clause in each sentence. Write _S_ (subject) or _SC_ (subject complement) to describe how each noun clause is used.

1. Our teacher's plan is that we will visit a museum of natural history. _____

2. My hope is that we will observe interesting displays about paleontology. _____

3. Whether we will see every exhibit about ancient animals is difficult to predict. _____

4. Where we might find reptile exhibits is the National Museum of Natural History. _____

5. The best part will be whatever I might learn about mammal and plant fossils. _____

6. A city bus and the subway were how we traveled to the museum. _____

7. The expansive rotunda area is where the class received a floor plan map. _____

8. Our first destination, the dinosaur hall, was where we observed their skeletons. _____

9. The most amazing sight is what we viewed in the impressive main hall. _____

10. How scientists acquired the immense giant squid specimen was my question. _____

11. My friend's favorite exhibit is what is displayed throughout the butterfly hall. _____

12. The museum guide, Mr. Stone, is who assists us in the fascinating fossil lab. _____

13. At the end of the day, it appears that everyone thoroughly enjoyed the field trip. _____

Complete each sentence with a noun clause used as a subject or a subject complement.

14. My favorite field trip was _____.

15. _____ is a paleontologist's biggest worry.

16. The importance of the trip is _____.

17. _____ was our chaperone's main fear.

18. A safety procedure on the bus is _____.

19. The dominant theme in many exhibits was _____.

20. My reaction to the museum was _____.

21. _____ is a concern for future field trips.

© Loyola Press. Voyages in English Grade 8

For additional help, review pages 152–153 in your textbook or visit www.voyagesinenglish.com.

8.8 Noun Clauses as Appositives

A noun clause can be used as an appositive. An appositive is a word or group of words that follows a noun and renames it or gives more information about it.

Underline the noun clause used as an appositive in each sentence. Circle the noun each clause renames.

1. The theme that hatred leads to tragedy is central to the play *Romeo and Juliet*.
2. The tradition that Romeo's and Juliet's families must fight does not keep the teens apart.
3. Romeo, however, maintains the belief that love will conquer all.
4. Juliet must hide the fact that she and Romeo were married in secret.
5. The friar has the knowledge that the marriage might be dangerous.
6. Juliet appears to be dead, so the truth that she took a sleeping potion isn't known immediately.
7. Unfortunately, Romeo believes the rumor that Juliet has died.
8. The tragedy that Romeo and Juliet both die at the end brings the families together.

Complete each sentence with a noun clause used as an appositive.

9. It was an excellent idea _____.
10. My hope _____ might be unrealistic.
11. The movie's theme _____ relates to Romeo and Juliet.
12. The audience's assumption _____ was quite mistaken.
13. Fortunately, my concern _____ was short-lived.
14. This actor's challenge _____ seems impossible.
15. One critic's opinion _____ made me wonder about the movie.
16. Other movies _____ might be set in present time periods.
17. I departed from the movie theater with the idea _____.

Write a sentence that includes a noun clause used as an appositive to rename each noun.

18. promise _____
19. thought _____
20. topic _____
21. request _____

8.9   Noun Clauses as Direct Objects

A noun clause can act as a direct object, which receives the action of the verb and answers the question *who* or *what* after the verb.

Underline the direct object in each sentence. Write *noun* or *noun clause* to identify each direct object.

1. I'll choose whatever looks best on me.   _____

2. Chelsea invited whoever wanted to attend the party.   _____

3. Most people take a camera when they go on vacation.   _____

4. Mateo wondered how he could try out for two sports.   _____

5. Justin suggested that we paint the room green.   _____

6. I wanted flowers rather than vegetables in the garden.   _____

7. Many people claimed that they did not enjoy the movie.   _____

8. Ian asked Bianca for help with the spaghetti dinner.   _____

9. Mom requested that we help her plant a vegetable garden.   _____

10. Penny will perform whichever is the best song for the show.   _____

11. My family discussed how we would spend summer vacation.   _____

12. We decided that we would wait until noon to go to the beach.   _____

13. I prefer humorous or historical movies.   _____

14. Keisha realized that she should have studied harder for the test. _____

Complete each sentence with a noun clause used as a direct object.

15. Tom studied _____.

16. Our coach explains _____.

17. The custodian noticed _____.

18. She did not understand _____.

19. During class we will discuss _____.

20. The newspaper club reported _____.

21. Their parents' organization contributed _____.

22. This afternoon the principal announced _____.

23. That company only insures _____.

For additional help, review pages 156–157 in your textbook or visit www.voyagesinenglish.com.

8.10 Noun Clauses as Objects of Prepositions

A noun clause can act as an object of a preposition.

Underline the noun clause used as an object of a preposition in each sentence. Then circle the preposition that introduces each noun clause.

1. My friends talked about what were the most violent kinds of storms.

2. Jake told us about what is known as the F-5 tornado.

3. A tornado's power is ranked by whatever its wind speed is.

4. The F-5 is a tornado with what are considered devastating winds.

5. Most tornadoes occur in what is known as the Midwest's Tornado Alley.

6. In this area people learn about how they can survive these storms.

7. People tell frightening stories about what they've seen during the storms.

8. Warm, moist air is driven east by what has developed into a cold front behind it.

Underline the noun clause in each sentence. Write *DO* (direct object) or *OP* (object of a preposition) to identify how the noun clause is used.

9. In 2008 Illinois was the site of what was an unusual weather event. _____

10. A rare winter tornado crashed through where unsuspecting towns existed. _____

11. Tornados usually do not occur around when the winter air is cold and dry. _____

12. The weather service stated that a January tornado happened once before. _____

13. A tornado damaged homes and barns by how it traveled through two towns. _____

14. A sheriff first noticed that a tornado landed in the afternoon near Poplar Grove. _____

15. The sudden storm damaged 12 cars by where the freight train was located. _____

16. Only a few people experienced what could be considered minor injuries. _____

Complete each sentence with a noun clause used as an object of the preposition.

17. Many people donate clothing to _____.

18. New plans were made for _____.

19. Numerous news articles were written about _____.

20. A list of necessary jobs was distributed to _____.

21. Some people are well prepared for _____.

For additional help, review pages 158–159 in your textbook or visit www.voyagesinenglish.com.

8.11 Simple, Compound, and Complex Sentences

A **simple sentence** is a single independent clause. A **compound sentence** contains two or more independent clauses. A **complex sentence** has one independent clause and at least one dependent clause.

Write *simple*, *compound*, or *complex* to identify each sentence. Underline each dependent clause. Circle the conjunction in each compound sentence.

1. Have you ever wondered about the formation of a rainbow?   _____

2. The process that creates a rainbow is actually quite simple.   _____

3. When the conditions are right, sunlight passes through drops of water in the air.   _____

4. Each drop of water acts like a miniature prism.   _____

5. Sunlight bends while passing through each drop, and the light separates into seven distinct colors.   _____

6. If you want to see a rainbow, the sun must be behind you.   _____

7. The water source must be in front of you.   _____

8. The water source itself is not important, but you will usually see rainbows after the rain.   _____

9. You will see fewer rainbows during the winter, although it's possible to see them year-round.   _____

Use the information in parentheses to rewrite each pair of simple sentences as a compound or a complex sentence.

10. Descartes studied rainbows. He analyzed the effect of light on a water droplet. (complex)

_____

11. Isaac Newton read about these studies of light. He experimented with prisms. (compound)

_____

12. Rainbows seem to contain only seven colors. Each is a blended range of colors. (complex)

_____

13. Sometimes a secondary rainbow is seen. Its colors appear in opposite order. (compound)

_____

© Loyola Press. Voyages in English   **Grade 8**

For additional help, review pages 160–161 in your textbook or visit www.voyagesinenglish.com.

SECTION 9 | Daily Maintenance

9.1 **The necklace with diamonds is beautiful, but I want these pearl earrings.**
1. Is the sentence simple, compound, or complex? _____
2. Is the sentence declarative or interrogative? _____
3. What is the adjective phrase? _____
4. Which word is a subject complement? _____
5. Diagram the sentence on another sheet of paper.

9.2 **Armando is wearing a shirt that he bought in Hawaii.**
1. Is the sentence declarative or imperative? _____
2. What is the adjective clause? _____
3. Which word does the adjective clause describe? _____
4. What is the independent clause? _____
5. Diagram the sentence on another sheet of paper.

9.3 **Did you recognize the author who was signing books?**
1. Is the sentence imperative or interrogative? _____
2. What is the adjective clause? _____
3. Is this clause restrictive or nonrestrictive? _____
4. Which words are used as direct objects? _____
5. Diagram the sentence on another sheet of paper.

9.4 **If you need a ride to school, I can take you.**
1. Is the sentence simple, compound, or complex? _____
2. What is the subordinate conjunction? _____
3. What is the adverb clause? _____
4. What is the independent clause? _____
5. Diagram the sentence on another sheet of paper.

9.5 **That Liz is a talented musician is obvious.**
1. Is the sentence simple, compound, or complex? _____
2. What is the noun clause? _____
3. Is it used as a subject or subject complement? _____
4. What is the introductory word of the clause? _____
5. Diagram the sentence on another sheet of paper.

9.6 **I can see that we need more sources for our report.**
1. Is the sentence simple, compound, or complex? _____
2. What is the verb phrase? _____
3. What is the object of the preposition? _____
4. What is the adjective phrase? _____
5. Diagram the sentence on another sheet of paper.

9.1 Coordinating Conjunctions

A **conjunction** is a word used to connect words or groups of words. A **coordinating conjunction** joins words or groups of words that are similar. The coordinating conjunctions are *and*, *but*, *or*, *nor*, *so*, and *yet*.

Circle the coordinating conjunction in each sentence. Underline the words, phrases, or clauses that each conjunction connects.

1. An amazing and unexpected discovery of gold coins occurred in Israel in 2008.
2. Nadine Ross was a British archaeologist, yet she located the coins near Jerusalem.
3. While working, Ms. Ross expected to unearth only glass or pottery at the site.
4. No pottery shards appeared near the coins, so the coins likely were hidden within walls.
5. The face of the coins depicted an ancient emperor in military clothes and holding a cross.
6. They probably were minted in the seventh century, but before the Byzantine era ended.
7. These coins denote one of the most extensive and significant archaeological finds in Israel.

Circle the coordinating conjunction to complete each sentence. Then write whether each connects *words*, *phrases*, or *clauses*.

8. Jenna planned to ski in the morning (and   but) in the afternoon. _____
9. We can paint the room sky blue (so   or) lemon yellow. _____
10. It is raining outside, (so   nor) we won't go to the beach. _____
11. Cameron double-majored in English (or   and) in biology. _____
12. Bailey couldn't decide between carrots (and   or) spinach. _____
13. Should I take a plane (but   or) a train to travel to Orlando? _____
14. I tried to hear the speech, (but   nor) the crowd was too noisy. _____
15. This summer we will not vacation in Spain (and   nor) in Italy. _____
16. We took the long (nor   but) beautiful trail to the summit. _____
17. Our seats were far back, (or   yet) we could still see the stage. _____
18. We can't visit the museum today, (but   so) we can return tomorrow. _____
19. Kay couldn't find her cat, (but   nor) did she suspect where it was hiding. _____

Complete each sentence with a coordinating conjunction and an appropriate word, phrase, or clause, as indicated in parentheses.

20. An archaeologist's work is challenging _____. (word)
21. Scientists may find artifacts near the river _____. (phrase)
22. We earnestly dug in the sand, _____. (clause)

For additional help, review pages 166–167 in your textbook or visit www.voyagesinenglish.com.

Section 9 • 109

9.2 Correlative Conjunctions

Correlative conjunctions are used in pairs to connect words or groups of words that have equal importance in a sentence.

Circle the correlative conjunctions in each sentence.

1. Let's bring both corn and chicken to the neighborhood picnic.
2. Either Mindy or Mom will make the dessert.
3. I will neither play games nor go swimming.
4. Bianca not only acted in the play but also sang.
5. Whether a puppy or a kitten, a pet is what Annie wants.
6. Terrance will drive neither the truck nor the van.
7. Neither Lisa nor Eric can make it to class on time.
8. Both Michael and I will run in the marathon on Saturday.
9. Jason is buying not only the baseball but also the bat and mitt.
10. In case I am late, we can meet at either the restaurant or the museum.
11. Both Lexi and her sister are making desserts for the party.
12. Whether Shana will play the leading role or be the director's assistant is still undecided.

Write correlative conjunctions to complete each sentence.

13. The magic show included _____ card tricks _____ escape tricks.

14. _____ children _____ adults were mesmerized by the magician's performance.

15. Audience members chose seats in _____ the side _____ the front of the theater.

16. _____ the magician _____ his assistant would reveal the secrets of the tricks.

17. _____ I learn a coin trick _____ the locking-rings trick, I will amaze my friends.

Write two sentences about your school activities, using correlative conjunctions. Circle each correlative conjunction.

18. _____

_____

19. _____

_____

© Loyola Press. Voyages in English Grade 8

For additional help, review pages 168–169 in your textbook or visit www.voyagesinenglish.com.

9.3 Conjunctive Adverbs

A **conjunctive adverb** connects independent clauses and makes clear the relationship between the clauses. **Parenthetical expressions,** or **explanatory expressions,** are used in the same way as conjunctive adverbs.

Circle the correct conjunctive adverb or parenthetical expression to complete each sentence.

1. There is only one biscuit left; (however   on the contrary), Mom is making more.
2. Dad is firing up the barbecue; (therefore   finally), we should buy some steaks.
3. Lasagna is a spicy, delicious food; (for example   moreover), it's pretty good for you.
4. I didn't plant enough peas; (then   in fact), I didn't plant enough beans either.
5. The horse is not fully trained; (however   consequently), it's not ready for the show.
6. Jackson built an extra bedroom; (later   still), it became his home office.
7. Lou must paint the playhouse soon; (finally   otherwise), the boys will be too old to use it.
8. Min chose a college close to home; (thus   besides), she'll be home on weekends.
9. Finals were finished today; (besides   finally), summer has arrived.
10. Our house is in the mountains; (indeed   thus), it sits over 5,000 feet above sea level.
11. Fashion is important to Kate; (otherwise   likewise), it is also an interest of her twin sister's.
12. The county fair has great food; (furthermore   still), it provides wonderful entertainment.
13. Kaley would like to join the tennis team; (on the other hand   therefore), she is an outstanding volleyball player.
14. The lake is too deep for swimming; (nevertheless   besides), it's too cold outside.
15. I put a lot of salt on my popcorn; (therefore   however), I didn't want to eat it.

Rewrite each sentence, adding a conjunctive adverb or parenthetical expression and correcting the punctuation as needed.

16. In 1949 Mines Field faced a major change it became Los Angeles International Airport.

_____

17. Thousands of flights pass through here yearly it is the fifth busiest airport.

_____

18. The airport offers amenities for travelers shops and restaurants crowd the terminals.

_____

19. Downtown Los Angeles is near the airport major entertainment surrounds it.

_____

For additional help, review pages 170–171 in your textbook or visit www.voyagesinenglish.com.

9.3 Conjunctive Adverbs

A **conjunctive adverb** connects independent clauses and makes clear the relationship between the clauses. **Parenthetical expressions,** or **explanatory expressions,** are used in the same way as conjunctive adverbs.

Complete each sentence with an appropriate conjunctive adverb or parenthetical expression.

1. California's second-largest city is San Diego; _____, it has a small-town feel.

2. San Diego is a vibrant city; _____, life here often feels calm and relaxed.

3. Visitors like the warm climate; _____, residents enjoy their time in the sun.

4. Mexico lies to the south; _____, the Pacific Ocean borders the city's western edge.

5. The San Diego Zoo houses rare animals; _____, giant pandas reside there.

6. Many coastal activities are available; _____, surfing is just one possibility.

7. Hang gliding over the ocean is more challenging; _____, it can be exhilarating.

8. Teens enjoy skating on Madison Beach boardwalk; _____, biking is popular.

9. The Padres draw baseball fans to San Diego; _____, football fans enthusiastically attend Chargers games.

10. Some tourists avoid outdoor pursuits; _____, they delight in theaters and museums.

11. San Diego contains more than 15 museums; _____, guests have numerous and varied indoor options.

12. San Diego was the area's first settlement; _____, it is viewed as California's birthplace.

13. Mason Street School was San Diego's first one-room school; _____, this was the city's original public school.

14. The school is a historic landmark; _____, desks, textbooks, and teaching materials are authentic artifacts.

Complete each sentence with a conjunctive adverb or parenthetical expression and an appropriate clause. Add semicolons and commas where needed.

15. Our city holds events for families _____.

16. We spend Sundays at soccer games _____.

17. I enjoy exploring the aquarium _____.

18. The historic building was once a barn _____.

19. We like to fly kites by the lake _____.

© Loyola Press. Voyages in English   Grade 8

For additional help, review pages 170–171 in your textbook or visit www.voyagesinenglish.com.

9.4 Subordinate Conjunctions

A **subordinate conjunction** joins an independent clause and a dependent clause and indicates their relationship. A subordinate conjunction may introduce an adverb clause, an adjective clause, or a noun clause.

Circle each subordinate conjunction and underline each dependent clause. Not all the sentences have subordinate conjunctions or dependent clauses.

1. When Jackie Robinson was asked to play in the American professional baseball leagues, he was the first African American to do so.

2. Before Robinson took this step, African Americans played in the Negro Leagues.

3. When Robinson signed his contract with the Brooklyn Dodgers in 1945, he broke the "color barrier."

4. As long as this barrier existed, sports would continue to have teams based on color.

5. Robinson rose to this exceptional challenge so that others could have opportunities.

6. Although he dealt with racism on a daily basis, Robinson showed great courage and persistence.

7. Jackie Robinson proved to everyone that he belonged in the majors.

8. In 1946 and 1947 Robinson won the National League batting title.

9. He triumphed again in 1949 when he was named the league's most valuable player.

10. Robinson set many league records as he played out his career with the Dodgers.

Underline the connector in each sentence. Write whether the connector is a conjunctive adverb (CA) or a subordinate conjunction (SC).

11. Often an athlete's story is told in order that we will be inspired to succeed. _____

12. A professional athlete struggles to recover from an injury; likewise, my friend strives to recover from a serious illness. _____

13. While pros make sports seem easy, they spend long hours honing their skills. _____

14. After I studied the tips in the DVD, my golf game improved noticeably. _____

15. Famous athletes run summer camps for youth; indeed, the athletes help campers learn new skills and techniques. _____

Write three sentences about an accomplished athlete or other famous person. Use a subordinate conjunction in each sentence.

16. _____

17. _____

18. _____

For additional help, review pages 172–173 in your textbook or visit www.voyagesinenglish.com.

9.5 Troublesome Conjunctions

Some conjunctions are frequently misused or confused.

Write a conjunction or a preposition from the box to correctly complete each sentence.

without	unless	like	as if	as

1. Justin found it difficult to see the board _____ his glasses.
2. _____ you put on your coat, you will get wet in the rain.
3. Elena looks _____ she has been up all night studying.
4. No one should venture outside in the snow _____ sturdy boots.
5. That lion looks _____ my oldest cat.
6. We sent a small gift _____ a special thank-you to our coach.
7. Does this candy taste _____ watermelon?
8. _____ an excuse from the doctor, you will be marked absent.
9. Shari ran _____ she were being chased by wild horses.
10. I held on to my hat _____ the wind whipped around me.
11. Please don't walk after dark _____ you have a friend with you.
12. My mom's banana bread is _____ no one else's.
13. Jim acted _____ he had won the ultimate prize.

Underline the conjunction in each sentence. Then complete the sentence with a prepositional phrase or a clause, as needed.

14. People should not hike in the mountains without _____.
15. My teacher smiled as if _____.
16. Our pet hamster will not eat unless _____.
17. We will use the study guide as _____.
18. You should not open the door unless _____.
19. I look a lot like _____.
20. Those children can't go one day without _____.
21. I hurried to the library as _____.

For additional help, review pages 174–175 in your textbook or visit www.voyagesinenglish.com.

9.5   Troublesome Conjunctions

Some conjunctions are frequently misused or confused.

Circle the correct item or items to complete each sentence. If the circled item is a subordinate conjunction, underline the clause it introduces.

1. The sport of lacrosse would not exist (without   unless) Native Americans.

2. Some Native Americans played games of lacrosse (like   as if) they were at war.

3. Young men developed strength and agility (as   like) they played this game.

4. Sometimes hundreds of players would compete for days (without   unless) a break.

5. At times this game was also played (as   like) part of ancient healing rituals.

6. Native people revered the game (as if   like) it possessed mystical and spiritual qualities.

7. These early forms of lacrosse differed from other stick sports (as   like) field hockey.

8. The Native American athletes attached a net on the stick (as if   as) a trap for the ball.

9. The accounts of those games came from people (like   as) missionaries and explorers.

10. In 1636 Jean de Brebeuf described lacrosse (as   like) a basic part of Native American life.

11. (Without   Unless) we recognize these writings, we can't appreciate the history of lacrosse.

12. A standard version (as if   like) the native game was devised by a Canadian dentist in 1867.

13. Modern leagues and teams could not have formed (unless   as) consistent rules were developed.

14. Before the 1930s men and women played lacrosse (unless   without) protective gear (like   as) the early Native Americans.

15. (As   As if) lacrosse is played throughout the United States today, many are amazed to learn of its reputation (like   as) the oldest sport in North America.

Use each word in a sentence. Include a prepositional phrase or a clause.

16. unless _____

17. without _____

18. as _____

19. like _____

20. as if _____

For additional help, review pages 174–175 in your textbook or visit www.voyagesinenglish.com.

9.6   Interjections

An **interjection** is a word that expresses a strong or sudden emotion. It is also used to get or hold attention.

Underline the interjection in each sentence. Then write another sentence using the same interjection. Use commas and exclamation marks as needed.

1. Yes, I would love to go ice-skating!

   _____

2. Oh no, the rain is really pouring down!

   _____

3. Ouch! I hit my knee on the corner of the coffee table.

   _____

4. Hush! After a long night, the baby is finally sleeping.

   _____

5. Hooray, they scored another touchdown!

   _____

6. No! Don't let the dog chew on those slippers.

   _____

7. Wow, that show was amazing!

   _____

8. Beware! That box of supplies is extremely heavy.

   _____

9. Hey! Move your car out of the way.

   _____

On another sheet of paper, write a sentence with an interjection that relates to each situation. Indicate the emotion that is expressed in each one.

10. drinking a cup of hot chocolate   13. spotting a spider

11. looking at a rainbow after a storm   14. accidentally ripping a page in a book

12. searching for a friend's lost pet   15. waving to a friend across the street

© Loyola Press. Voyages in English   Grade 8

For additional help, review pages 176–177 in your textbook or visit www.voyagesinenglish.com.

SECTION 10 Daily Maintenance

10.1 **A shirt or a tie is a good gift for my father.**
1. Is the sentence simple, compound, or complex? _____
2. What is the coordinating conjunction? _____
3. Which word is the subject complement? _____
4. What is the adjective phrase? _____
5. Diagram the sentence on another sheet of paper.

10.2 **Richard did not study for the science test; therefore, he earned a low score.**
1. Is the sentence simple, compound, or complex? _____
2. What is the conjunctive adverb? _____
3. What is the adverb phrase? _____
4. What is the antecedent of the pronoun *he*? _____
5. Diagram the sentence on another sheet of paper.

10.3 **When I lived in Arizona, I often visited the Colorado River.**
1. Is the sentence simple, compound, or complex? _____
2. What is the subordinate conjunction? _____
3. What is the adverb clause? _____
4. Which word is an adverb? _____
5. Diagram the sentence on another sheet of paper.

10.4 **Lola cannot go unless her parents give their permission.**
1. Is the sentence simple, compound, or complex? _____
2. What is the subordinate conjunction? _____
3. Does it introduce an adjective or adverb clause? _____
4. Which words are possessive adjectives? _____
5. Diagram the sentence on another sheet of paper.

10.5 **Bravo, your performance in the play was superb!**
1. What is the adjective phrase? _____
2. What is the linking verb? _____
3. What part of speech is the subject complement? _____
4. What is the interjection? _____
5. Diagram the sentence on another sheet of paper.

© Loyola Press. Voyages in English   Grade 8

10.1 Periods and Commas

A **period** is used at the end of a declarative or an imperative sentence, after an abbreviation, and after initials. **Commas** are used in a variety of ways to separate or set off words.

Rewrite each sentence to correct any errors in punctuation.

1. Collene the guests are beginning to arrive

   _____

2. "Sir you forgot your coat" Tanya announced to Mr Chang

   _____

3. "I need" Dad continued "some help with these dishes"

   _____

4. Many people like St Louis Missouri and I am one of them

   _____

5. Mrs Davis asked "How many, students want to go on the field trip?"

   _____

6. I can't decide whether to visit San Diego California or Dallas Texas

   _____

7. His full name which is known only to his friends is Charles S Winslow

   _____

8. Shane my little brother was born on, Monday June 7 2004 at lunchtime.

   _____

9. At 8:00 a m our director Ms Jenna Langer will post the new cast list

   _____

10. I had not read any J K Rowling books; nonetheless I did enjoy the movies

    _____

11. Alana, Sam and Trey placed first, second and third, so I heard in the spelling bee

    _____

12. The children were tired yet they did not want to go to sleep

    _____

For additional help, review pages 182–183 in your textbook or visit www.voyagesinenglish.com.

Section 10 • 119

10.2 Exclamation Points, Question Marks, Semicolons, and Colons

> **Exclamation points** are used after interjections and exclamatory sentences. **Question marks** are used to end interrogative sentences. **Semicolons** and **colons** are used in specific situations.

Rewrite the following sentences with the correct punctuation.

1. Hooray Finally summer had arrived.

   _____

2. Should I visit my grandparents during spring break.

   _____

3. Brian carried the boxes upstairs they were very heavy.

   _____

4. Yes. This was going to be the best summer ever.

   _____

5. I couldn't wait to get started however, I didn't know what to do first

   _____

6. "Dear Doctor Schwartz" is how my letter requesting information began.

   _____

7. I might work at an animal shelter namely, Animal Avenue, where my friend volunteers.

   _____

8. My work schedule is as follows Monday morning, Thursday afternoon, and Friday night.

   _____

9. My grandparents' birthdates are March 23, 1937 July 3, 1932 and March 4 1936.

   _____

On another sheet of paper, use each topic to write a sentence that includes the punctuation mark in parentheses.

10. an important event at school (exclamation point)

11. a friend's favorite school subject (question mark)

12. choices for after-school activities (semicolon or colon)

© Loyola Press. Voyages in English   Grade 8

For additional help, review pages 184–185 in your textbook or visit www.voyagesinenglish.com.

10.3   Quotation Marks and Italics

Quotation marks are used with direct quotations and to set off titles of stories, magazine articles, and radio programs. **Single quotation marks** are used within a quotation. **Italics** are used for the titles of some items.

Rewrite each sentence. Use quotation marks and underlining to indicate italics where needed.

1. Did you read this article in today's L.A. Times? Dad asked.

   _____

2. Please, my little sister begged, let me go with you to the mall.

   _____

3. Did Christopher Columbus sail on the Niña, the Pinta, or the Santa Maria?

   _____

4. Have you read the story Lost in Memphis? my teacher asked.

   _____

5. This story, Mr. Loomis said, is based on the poem Among the Leaves.

   _____

6. The Queen Elizabeth 2 is one of the world's largest passenger ships.

   _____

7. Did you see the movie To Touch the Sky: Climbing Mt. Everest last summer?

   _____

8. Can you relate your life to The Road Not Taken by Robert Frost? asked Mr. Moore.

   _____

9. The book Renaissance Artists has a picture of Leonardo da Vinci's painting The Last Supper.

   _____

10. You can find the article Tennis Legends in this month's Sports Illustrated for Kids.

    _____

11. The lyrics for The Star-Spangled Banner can be found in American Songbook.

    _____

12. Amazing Animal Rescues is my favorite television series! exclaimed Troy.

    _____

For additional help, review pages 186–187 in your textbook
or visit www.voyagesinenglish.com.

10.4 Apostrophes, Hyphens, and Dashes

Apostrophes, hyphens, and **dashes** are used to clarify text for the reader.

Fill in the circle in front of the answer that shows the correct punctuation for each item.

1. the Smiths dog
   - ○ the Smith's dog
   - ○ the Smiths dog's
   - ○ the Smiths' dog

2. words with *us* and *os*
   - ○ words with *us'* and *os'*
   - ○ words with *u's* and *o's*
   - ○ words with *u's* and *os*

3. twenty five years worth
   - ○ twenty-five year's worth
   - ○ twenty five years' worth
   - ○ twenty-five years' worth

4. sixth graders graduation
   - ○ sixth-graders graduation
   - ○ sixth-graders' graduation
   - ○ sixth grader's graduation

5. Im in the class of 09.
   - ○ I'm in the class of '09.
   - ○ I'm in the class of 09.
   - ○ I'm in the class of "09."

6. my mother in laws purse
   - ○ my mother-in laws' purse
   - ○ my mother's-in-law purse
   - ○ my mother-in-law's purse

7. the forty two cats of the Joneses
   - ○ the Jone's fortytwo cats
   - ○ the Joneses' forty-two cats
   - ○ the Jones' forty-two cats

8. the Unions flag in 63
   - ○ the Unions' flag in "63"
   - ○ the Unions flag in '63
   - ○ the Union's flag in '63

9. Shes a nine year old girl.
   - ○ Shes a nine-year-old-girl.
   - ○ She's a nine-year-old girl.
   - ○ She's a nine year old girl.

10. three *bs* and two *Ds* in my name
    - ○ three *b's* and two *Ds* in my name
    - ○ three *bs* and two *D's* in my name
    - ○ three *b's* and two *D's* in my name

Rewrite each sentence, using apostrophes, hyphens, and dashes correctly.

11. Well never forget our high schools ten year reunion.

    _____

12. The childrens first aid kit we found it under the sink really came in handy.

    _____

13. Marys favorite dishes lasagna, chicken piccata, and spinach salad were at the buffet.

    _____

© Loyola Press. Voyages in English   Grade 8

For additional help, review pages 188–189 in your textbook or visit www.voyagesinenglish.com.

10.5 | Capitalization

> Using **capital letters** correctly provides valuable clues for the reader that make your writing easier to understand.

Rewrite each sentence, using correct capitalization.

1. my favorite book is <u>little house on the prairie</u> by laura ingalls wilder.

   _____

2. yesterday aunt celene exclaimed, "this book was one of my favorites too!"

   _____

3. while reading the book, i learned a lot about what life was like in america long ago.

   _____

4. i was interested to discover how the ingalls family survived on the Prairie.

   _____

5. she describes her travels to independence, kansas, in a covered wagon.

   _____

6. i would have been frightened to travel to unknown lands in the west.

   _____

7. my favorite part was when they met the native americans.

   _____

8. i read the book as an english assignment, but i'll have read the whole Series by Summer.

   _____

9. I plan to read more books by ms. wilder describing her life throughout the united states.

   _____

10. The laura ingalls wilder historic home and museum shows where she lived while writing.

    _____

Write a sentence that gives your name, date, and place of birth.

_____

_____

For additional help, review pages 190–191 in your textbook or visit www.voyagesinenglish.com.

SECTION 11 Daily Maintenance

11.1 Mike handed his sister the smallest kitten in the litter.
1. How is the word *sister* used in the sentence?   _____
2. What kind of adjective describes *kitten*?   _____
3. How is the word *kitten* used in the sentence?   _____
4. What is the adjective phrase?   _____
5. Diagram the sentence on another sheet of paper.

11.2 A kimono, a long robe with a sash, is a Japanese garment.
1. What is the appositive?   _____
2. Is it restrictive or nonrestrictive?   _____
3. Which noun is the object of a preposition?   _____
4. How is the word *garment* used in the sentence?   _____
5. Diagram the sentence on another sheet of paper.

11.3 The students have learned their parts, and now they will rehearse the play.
1. Is the sentence simple, compound, or complex?   _____
2. Which word is a coordinating conjunction?   _____
3. Which words are direct objects?   _____
4. Which word is an adverb?   _____
5. Diagram the sentence on another sheet of paper.

11.4 The young children built a sand castle and decorated it with shells.
1. What is the complete subject?   _____
2. Is the subject or the predicate compound?   _____
3. What is the antecedent of the word *it*?   _____
4. Which plural noun is irregular?   _____
5. Diagram the sentence on another sheet of paper.

11.5 **The tall man standing beside my sister is her husband.**
1. What is the simple subject? _____
2. What is the participial phrase? _____
3. Does it act as an adjective or an adverb? _____
4. Which word is a subject complement? _____
5. Diagram the sentence on another sheet of paper.

11.6 **Working in my vegetable garden is a relaxing pastime for me.**
1. Which word is a gerund? _____
2. How is the gerund phrase used in the sentence? _____
3. Which word is a participial adjective? _____
4. What is the subject complement? _____
5. Diagram the sentence on another sheet of paper.

11.7 **Her suggestion, to invite local artists to the class, excited the art students.**
1. What is the simple predicate? _____
2. How is the infinitive used in the sentence? _____
3. What is the prepositional phrase? _____
4. What kind of adjective is the word *Her*? _____
5. Diagram the sentence on another sheet of paper.

11.8 **These are the people who earned the highest scores on the math quiz.**
1. What kind of pronoun is the word *These*?   _____
2. What is the subject complement?   _____
3. How is the word *scores* used in the sentence?   _____
4. What does the adjective clause describe?   _____
5. Diagram the sentence on another sheet of paper.

11.9 **Phil is relieved because someone found his missing keys.**
1. How is the word *relieved* used in the sentence?   _____
2. Is the adverb clause dependent or independent?   _____
3. What is the antecedent of the word *his*?   _____
4. What kind of pronoun is the word *someone*?   _____
5. Diagram the sentence on another sheet of paper.

11.10 **We learned that some butterflies migrate to warmer climates in winter months.**
1. What are the person and number of *We*?   _____
2. How is the noun clause used in the sentence?   _____
3. What kind of adjective is the word *some*?   _____
4. Which words are objects of prepositions?   _____
5. Diagram the sentence on another sheet of paper.

11.11 **My goal, becoming an astronaut, requires years of hard work and dedication.**
1. What is the complete subject?   _____
2. What is the gerund?   _____
3. How is the gerund phrase used in the sentence?   _____
4. Which words are abstract nouns?   _____
5. Diagram the sentence on another sheet of paper.

11.1 Simple Sentences

A **diagram** is a visual outline of a sentence. It shows in a graphic manner the relationships among the various words or groups of words in a sentence.

Diagram the sentences.

1. Last week my brother bought a gold watch.

2. The paintings in the university gallery were amazing.

3. Our school's student council proudly declared the event a huge success.

4. At bedtime Joey read his younger sister a story from the new book.

For additional help, review pages 196–197 in your textbook or visit www.voyagesinenglish.com.

Section 11 • 127

11.2   Appositives

An **appositive** is a word or a group of words that follows a noun or a pronoun and further identifies it or adds information. An appositive names the same person, place, thing, or idea as the word it explains.

Diagram the sentences.

1. Terrance, my older brother, plays college football.

2. We watched the movie *Sounder* over the weekend.

3. The class read a novel by F. Scott Fitzgerald, an American author.

4. The cellist Yo-Yo Ma played at the Hollywood Bowl, a famous amphitheater in Los Angeles.

© Loyola Press. Voyages in English   Grade 8

For additional help, review pages 198–199 in your textbook or visit www.voyagesinenglish.com.

11.3 Compound Sentences

A **compound sentence** contains two or more independent clauses. An independent clause has a subject and a predicate and can stand on its own as a sentence.

Diagram the sentences.

1. I easily remembered my backpack, yet I forgot my new camera.

2. Justin ate four sandwiches; afterwards, he had two pieces of pie.

3. The rain poured down on us, but we finished the baseball game anyway.

4. My sister Shari majored in English; in fact, she has two degrees in modern literature.

© Loyola Press. Voyages in English   Grade 8

For additional help, review pages 200–201 in your textbook or visit www.voyagesinenglish.com.

Section 11 • 129

11.4 Compound Sentence Elements

The subject and the predicate in a sentence may be compound. They may consist of two or more words connected by a coordinating conjunction. A sentence with these compound elements is still a simple sentence.

Diagram the sentences.

1. Sara and her grandmother planted tomatoes in the vegetable garden.

2. That young artist sketched and painted the pictures for the art fair.

3. Over the rainy weekend, my best friend and I watched movies and played board games.

4. The town hall meeting at the community center was interesting and very informative.

© Loyola Press. Voyages in English Grade 8

For additional help, review pages 202–203 in your textbook or visit www.voyagesinenglish.com.

11.5 Participles

A **participle** is a verbal that is used as an adjective. A participial phrase is made up of the participle and its objects, complements, and any modifiers. The entire phrase acts as an adjective.

Diagram the sentences.

1. Sophia entered her pie, baked to perfection, in the contest.

2. Resting on the beach, Ryan listened to the crashing waves.

3. The elephant, reaching our hands with its trunk, took some peanuts.

4. My softball team, having won the playoffs, threw a huge celebration party.

For additional help, review pages 204–205 in your textbook or visit www.voyagesinenglish.com.

11.6 Gerunds

A **gerund** is a verb form ending in *ing* that is used as a noun. A gerund can be used in a sentence as a subject, a subject complement, an object of a verb, an object of a preposition, or an appositive.

Diagram the sentences.

1. My entire family enjoys watching old movies.

2. Climbing high points in each state is my aunt's favorite pastime.

3. This small book gives information about hiking local mountain trails.

4. His new hobby, constructing kites, consumes his free time on the weekend.

© Loyola Press. Voyages in English   Grade 8

For additional help, review pages 206–207 in your textbook or visit www.voyagesinenglish.com.

11.7 Infinitives

An **infinitive** is a verb form, usually preceded by *to,* that is used as a noun, an adjective, or an adverb.

Diagram the sentences.

1. The student's primary goal is to finish the history report by the due date.

2. Her original idea, to plan a surprise party, excited the whole family.

3. The neighbor at the end of the block has a room to rent.

4. Mr. Wilkins remembered to place the empty bottles on the front porch.

© Loyola Press. Voyages in English   Grade 8

For additional help, review pages 208–209 in your textbook or visit www.voyagesinenglish.com.

Section 11 • 133

11.8   Adjective Clauses

> An **adjective clause** is a dependent clause that describes or limits a noun or a pronoun.

Diagram the sentences.

1. My bike, which was bright red, has now been painted royal blue.

2. My cousin Taylor gave our grandfather the gift that she bought in China.

3. Annette was the composer whose song was chosen for the school play.

4. The announcement was made in the auditorium, where everyone was assembled.

© Loyola Press. Voyages in English   Grade 8

For additional help, review pages 210–211 in your textbook or visit www.voyagesinenglish.com.

11.9 Adverb Clauses

> An **adverb clause** is a dependent clause that acts as an adverb; it describes a verb, an adjective, or another adverb.

Diagram the sentences.

1. Since Keisha joined our class, discussions are much more interesting.

2. Although Carter loves the rain, he is afraid of thunderstorms.

3. We will show the slides when Lisa returns from her vacation.

4. The nature group hiked down the mountain before the sun had set.

For additional help, review pages 212–213 in your textbook or visit www.voyagesinenglish.com.

Section 11 • 135

11.10   Noun Clauses

Dependent clauses can be used as nouns. **Noun clauses** work in sentences in the same way that nouns do.

Diagram the sentences.

1. That he finished the program in three months is a remarkable achievement.

2. Carl's biggest concern is whether he can arrive at the airport on time.

3. This new set of directions clearly shows how the parts fit together.

4. My English teacher presented a homework pass to whoever read the most books.

For additional help, review pages 214–215 in your textbook or visit www.voyagesinenglish.com.

11.11 Diagramming Practice

Diagramming serves two purposes. First, it helps you to understand how a sentence is put together. Second, it identifies errors in a sentence and makes it clear why they are errors.

Read the diagram and write the sentence.

1.
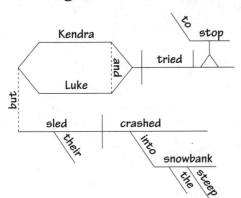

1. _____
   _____
   _____
   _____

2.
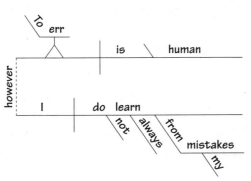

2. _____
   _____
   _____
   _____

3.

3. _____
   _____
   _____
   _____

4.
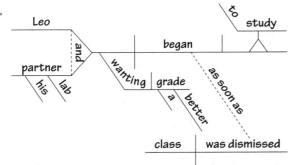

4. _____
   _____
   _____
   _____

For additional help, review pages 216–217 in your textbook
or visit www.voyagesinenglish.com.

What Makes a Good Personal Narrative?

A **personal narrative** is a first-person account of an incident in a writer's life. A good personal narrative demonstrates awareness of **audience,** has a clear **structure,** maintains **coherence,** and has an engaging **title.**

Read the personal narrative. Then answer the questions.

Would it be all right? Could I do it? I had spent six long months learning the routine. It seemed every time I had performed the dance in rehearsal, I had made a mistake. Once I even fell down. But this time, with the spotlight brightly blinding me to the audience and my skin tingling, I felt myself dance as if I were in a dream. The music surged through me like blood, the pulsation of the drums keeping time with my pounding heart. Every step and move was perfect! I didn't just dance to the music, I was part of the music. It rushed to me and through me, and flowed out and over the auditorium.

1. Underline the sentence that identifies the topic. What effect do the questions in the introduction have on the reader?

   _____

2. How does the description of the dancer's previous troubles build coherence?

   _____

3. How does the author show awareness of audience?

   _____

4. How might a reader who has never danced relate to this narrative? What theme does it touch upon that is more significant than merely a dance performance?

   _____

   _____

5. What descriptive words make the narrative more interesting?

   _____

6. Would "My Dance Recital" or "Dancing the Dream" be a better title for this narrative? Why?

   _____

   _____

© Loyola Press. Voyages in English   Grade 8

For additional help, review pages 224–227 in your textbook or visit www.voyagesinenglish.com.

Introduction, Body, and Conclusion

The **introduction** of a personal narrative interests readers and sets
expectations. The **body** should be well organized and include concrete images
and sensory details. The **conclusion** leaves a final impression or message.

**Here are possible introductory sentences for a personal narrative. Write if each
would be an ineffective (*I*) or an effective (*E*) introductory sentence.**

1. Once I visited my uncle's apple orchard in upstate New York.   _____

2. After a deafening crash, all we heard was complete silence.   _____

3. Both the dog and I froze as we saw each other at exactly the same moment.   _____

4. A trip to the zoo is an educational experience.   _____

5. I expected to be bored visiting an exhibition of WWII airplanes with Granddad. _____

6. When do you keep a secret, and when must you break your word?   _____

7. The first day of camp was filled with activities.   _____

Write a vivid phrase using sensory details for each item.

8. the sound of traffic _____

9. the sight of snow _____

10. an insect bite _____

11. a surprising discovery _____

12. the smell of a favorite food _____

13. a sense of accomplishment _____

14. a feeling of fear _____

Read this idea for a personal narrative. Then answer the question.

A student, unhappy about moving to a new school, spends a confused
day lost and late to class. Some people are rude, while others ignore
the student. Miserable, the student gets help from a surprising source.

15. Write a conclusion that makes a statement, summarizes the experience, or leaves a strong
impression for readers.

_____

_____

_____

© Loyola Press. Voyages in English   Grade 8

For additional help, review pages 228–231 in your textbook
or visit www.voyagesinenglish.com.

Chapter 1 • 139

Time Lines

A **time line** helps a writer arrange events in chronological order. Time lines show incidents on a horizontal, vertical, or diagonal line in the order that they took place. **Transition words** help readers understand the flow of events.

Number these events of a hiking trip in the order that they occurred. Then use another sheet of paper to transfer the events to a time line.

A Hiking Disaster

1. I must have dropped our map as I packed up the trash. _____

2. Darkness fell and we began to get cold. _____

3. The cool morning gave way to warmth as we hiked. _____

4. Forest rangers found us shivering just after dawn. _____

5. We huddled fearfully, hearing sounds in the dark night. _____

6. We sat down by a pretty mountain stream for lunch. _____

7. Our flashlight batteries gave out some time after midnight. _____

8. First we met at the trailhead, ready to get started. _____

9. Now lost, we found our phones had no signal here. _____

10. We soon lost the trail but wandered hoping to find it. _____

Write transition words to improve the flow of these sentences.

11. I painted my room by myself, but _____ I had to get my parent's permission.

12. I took all the furniture out and _____ covered the floor with plastic.

13. _____, I repaired the small holes and cracks with plaster.

14. _____ that step, I painted the edges and corners.

15. _____ I finished the first coat, it looked splotchy.

16. _____ though, after it dried, it looked better.

17. I studied my hard work so far _____ my lunch break.

18. _____ the second coat, the walls looked much better.

19. _____ I waited for the second coat to dry, I cleaned up spatters.

20. _____, I showed my parents my "new" room.

21. It was a lot of work, but _____ it was worth it.

© Loyola Press. Voyages in English   Grade 8

For additional help, review pages 232–235 in your textbook or visit www.voyagesinenglish.com.

LESSON
4

Varied Sentences

> **Varied sentences** make writing more interesting. Sentences of various **lengths, types,** and **complexity** will keep your writing from becoming predictable or boring.

Write *S* for each simple sentence, *CD* for each compound sentence, and *CX* for each complex sentence.

1. The many features of new cell phones confuse some people. _____

2. While we were on the mountain road, the rangers closed the gates behind us. _____

3. The mirror on the dresser was faded, but the wood still gleamed beautifully. _____

4. I am riding my bike when I can because we should all do our part to save energy. _____

5. He could take the easy shot himself, or he could pass to his teammate. _____

6. Spring, with its riotous growth, is my favorite season. _____

Rewrite each pair of sentences as a compound sentence, using a coordinating conjunction. Delete or add words as needed.

7. My new computer came with an LCD screen. It also has a memory card reader.

_____

8. We could get there in time if we walked. We would have to leave home early.

_____

9. I didn't know where the store was in the mall. I didn't know the location of the restroom.

_____

Rewrite each pair of sentences as a complex sentence, using a subordinate conjunction. Delete or add words as needed.

10. Rocky Mountain National Park is home to a huge herd of elk. The park is near Estes Park, Colorado.

_____

11. I admit I sometimes buy designer clothes. I don't think they are a good value.

_____

12. She is taking French next term. Unfortunately she may have to drop choir.

_____

13. Sarah was quite pleased with my efforts. I didn't know it at the time.

_____

© Loyola Press. Voyages in English Grade 8

For additional help, review pages 236–239 in your textbook or visit www.voyagesinenglish.com.

Exact Words

Exact words create clear and vivid pictures in readers' minds. Replacing general words—nouns, verbs, adjectives, and adverbs—with more specific words enlivens your writing.

Write a more specific noun for each of these nouns. Use a thesaurus if necessary.

1. fish _____   6. tree _____

2. child _____   7. book _____

3. noise _____   8. rock _____

4. fruit _____   9. criminal _____

5. belief _____   10. house _____

Replace the verb *said* in each sentence with a more exact or interesting synonym.

11. "I just don't know about that boy," Mom *said.* _____

12. "You'd better get started on that assignment," Mr. Collins *said.* _____

13. He *said* _____ softly, "Don't let them hear you."

14. "That is truly hilarious," Amy *said.* _____

15. Lisa *said,* _____ "Don't open that door!"

16. "Please don't tell Mom I ate all the snacks," my little brother *said.* _____

Add adverbs or adjectives to each sentence as indicated in parentheses.

17. He scrubbed the sink until it gleamed like a jewel. (adjective)

_____

18. Samantha danced through the house when she presented her report card. (adverb)

_____

19. Cal's outfit was without question the topic in the hallway. (adjective)

_____

20. I advanced toward the barking dog. (adverb)

_____

21. The wind whistled through the limbs of the trees. (adjective)

_____

© Loyola Press. Voyages in English   Grade 8

For additional help, review pages 240–243 in your textbook or visit www.voyagesinenglish.com.

LESSON
1

What Makes a Good How-to Article?

A **how-to article** gives directions for doing something. Good how-to writing is appropriate for its audience. It introduces its topic clearly, has an organized body of text, and concludes by summarizing the end product or impact.

Imagine you are writing a how-to article called "Operating a Combination Lock" that will be used by students new to your school.

1. Write an introduction that clearly states the topic and purpose of this article.

   _____

   _____

2. Write a conclusion that summarizes what the expected result or outcome should be.

   _____

   _____

Think about the audience and purpose of this article. For each idea, write _A_ if it is appropriate or _I_ if it is inappropriate.

3. ____ the history of lockmaking

4. ____ what to do if you make a mistake on the dial

5. ____ where to put a combination lock

6. ____ the names of the parts of a combination lock

7. ____ the difference between clockwise and counterclockwise on the lock dial

8. ____ the best-selling brands of combination locks

9. ____ where to set the numbers to begin

On another sheet of paper, rewrite each statement or question as an imperative sentence for a how-to article.

10. The person twirls the dial three times clockwise.

11. The first number is then moved under the pointer.

12. Can you get the numbers lined up exactly?

13. Next, the dial moves backward a full circle.

14. Then the next number goes beneath the mark.

15. It is easy not to be careful and go too far.

16. The dial spins back to the last number and opens the lock.

For additional help, review pages 262–265 in your textbook or visit www.voyagesinenglish.com.

Chapter 2 • 143

Making Instructions Clear and Concise

The key to writing how-to articles is to **make instructions clear and concise**. Good organization, direct instruction, and helpful transition words, such as *first*, *then*, *next*, and *finally*, help readers follow your directions.

Write *1–10* to place these steps for making French toast in the correct order.

A. ____ Place the coated bread slice in the hot pan or on the griddle.

B. ____ Turn over the bread in the egg mixture so that both sides are coated.

C. ____ Finally, cover your French toast with butter, syrup, powdered sugar, fresh berries, whipped cream, or other toppings of your choice. Eat!

D. ____ In a bowl thoroughly mix together the eggs, vanilla, and milk.

E. ____ When the second side is done, place the toast on a serving plate.

F. ____ First, gather the ingredients: two eggs, 1/4 tsp. vanilla, 1/8 cup milk, a tablespoon of butter, and four slices of bread.

G. ____ Let the butter melt in a frying pan or on a griddle while you mix the ingredients.

H. ____ Place a slice of bread in the egg mixture.

I. ____ Flip the bread over after the first side is golden brown.

J. ____ Repeat for all four slices of bread.

Show where you would insert transition words to make the sequence of steps clear. Then rewrite the paragraph on another sheet of paper.

Starting a lawn tractor is easy enough, but doing it properly protects both you and the machine. Put on hearing protectors; over time, machine noise can damage your hearing. Make sure the machine is on level ground as you take your seat. Put the gearshift lever in neutral. Be sure that the blade control is off. With your left foot, push in the brake/clutch pedal. Pull out the choke lever from the dash. Adjust the throttle lever to about halfway. Turn the key to start the machine. Release the key when the engine starts. Wait about 30 seconds or until the engine starts to sputter. Push the choke control back in. Select the gear, or speed, you want. Gently let out the brake/clutch pedal and away you go.

For additional help, review pages 266–269 in your textbook or visit www.voyagesinenglish.com.

LESSON
3

Revising Sentences

When **revising sentences,** keep them clear and to the point. **Rambling sentences** have too many ideas in one sentence. **Run-on sentences** connect more than one independent clause without conjunctions or punctuation.

Read each sentence. Write *R* if the sentence is a rambling sentence. Write *X* if the sentence is a run-on sentence. Write *OK* if the sentence is correct.

1. Carving a pumpkin for a fall festival is not hard, though some people prefer to paint them and you have to be careful not to cut yourself or make a huge mess. _____

2. A larger pumpkin is easy to work with, but there's more material to be scooped from inside, and it will require more cleanup. _____

3. Small pumpkins are cute, sometimes it is hard to get your hand inside for carving or cleaning though. _____

4. Use a sharp knife but be careful and have a rag handy to keep the handle dry so it won't slip and also have old newspaper or a wastebasket right there. _____

5. Trace your design in pencil on the pumpkin; it doesn't have to be a face, although that is the most common design. _____

6. Carefully cut the lid next, be sure to make the edges jagged so that the lid won't fall inside the pumpkin. _____

7. Scoop out the pulp and seeds, this is messy, but just grin and bear it. _____

8. Carefully cut out the design you chose, using the tracing you made to guide you. _____

9. It may help to reach inside the pumpkin and pop pieces out or to cut just half a section at a time or to use a smaller knife for tight areas but be sure to work slowly. _____

10. Place a light in your pumpkin, put it in a safe place, stand back, enjoy the effect. _____

Rewrite correctly each run-on sentence. Add or delete words and punctuation as necessary.

11. _____

_____

12. _____

_____

13. _____

_____

14. _____

_____

© Loyola Press. Voyages in English   **Grade 8**

For additional help, review pages 270–273 in your textbook
or visit www.voyagesinenglish.com.

LESSON 4 Roots

Knowing the meaning of a word's **root** can help you understand it and other related words. Many roots are Latin or Greek in origin.

Write two words that are based on each root. Use a dictionary if necessary.

1. The Latin root *cred*, meaning "believe" _____

2. The Latin root *cap*, meaning "head" _____

3. The Greek root *psych*, meaning "mind" or "soul" _____

4. The Latin root *clar*, meaning "clear" _____

5. The Latin root *don*, meaning "give" _____

6. The Latin root *port*, meaning "carry" _____

7. The Greek root *phon*, meaning "sound" _____

8. The Latin root *tex*, meaning "weave" _____

9. The Latin root *div*, meaning "divide" _____

10. The Greek root *opt*, meaning "eye" _____

Underline the root common to each word pair. Then use a dictionary to find the meaning of the root.

11. mania, pyromaniac _____

12. unison, sonata _____

13. voracious, carnivore _____

14. regime, regulate _____

15. tactile, contact _____

16. amateur, amiable _____

17. tripod, podiatrist _____

18. novel, innovate _____

19. lithograph, neolithic _____

The Greek root *ology* means "the study of" or "the science of." Write five or more words that are based on this root.

_____

_____

© Loyola Press. Voyages in English   Grade 8

For additional help, review pages 274–277 in your textbook or visit www.voyagesinenglish.com.

Dictionary

A **dictionary** is a writer's most important tool. Dictionary entries provide information on syllabication, pronunciation, definition, part of speech, usage, etymology (origin), and other forms or meanings.

Find each word in a dictionary. Show the correct syllabication of each word.

1. diagonal _____
2. magic _____
3. flagrant _____
4. estimate _____

5. current _____
6. inviolable _____
7. separate _____
8. dictionary _____

Use a dictionary to identify two possible parts of speech and their meanings for each word. Write a sentence using the word in each of these two ways.

9. separate

_____

_____

10. contract

_____

_____

11. vault

_____

_____

Use a dictionary, either online or in book form, to understand the meaning of each word. Then write a more common synonym for each word.

12. pallid _____
13. rend _____
14. flagrant _____
15. inhibit _____
16. naive _____
17. conundrum _____
18. congregate _____
19. despondent _____

20. gamut _____
21. requisite _____
22. ritual _____
23. venerate _____
24. transpire _____
25. adjudicate _____
26. enunciate _____
27. predicament _____

© Loyola Press. Voyages in English   Grade 8

For additional help, review pages 278–281 in your textbook or visit www.voyagesinenglish.com.

What Makes a Good Business Letter?

A **business letter** is a formal letter with a business-related purpose. To make it effective, business letters are confident, polite, and concise. A business letter includes a heading, an inside address, a salutation, the body, and a closing.

Complete the sentences to tell about each part of an effective business letter.

1. The opening paragraph should contain _____

_____.

2. The middle paragraphs need to _____

_____.

3. The closing paragraph should _____

_____.

Write the correct salutation for the following positions, related specifically to people in your community, region, or state.

4. Your state's U.S. senator: _____

5. Your community's mayor: _____

Rewrite this heading and inside address to show the correct form for a business letter.

November 15, 20—

Chute Middle School
1850 Oakton St., Evanston, IL 60202
(847) 555-0099

The Field Museum, Dr. Samuel Smith
1400 S. Lake Shore Drive
Chicago, IL 60605

On another sheet of paper, use the addresses above to write a short business letter to the museum, requesting information about an upcoming exhibit.

For additional help, review pages 300–303 in your textbook or visit www.voyagesinenglish.com.

LESSON
2

Purpose and Tone

A good business letter should state the **purpose** clearly and support it with relevant details. The letter's **tone** should be polite and sincere but not too formal or overly casual.

Read the passage. Then follow the directions or answer the questions.

I want to express my disappointment in a recent visit to Blue Water Adventure Park and request a refund of my admission price. Dude, would you want to stand in line for two hours? Well, guess what? That's what happened because three of the rides were busted. When my brother and I bought our tickets, no one told us any rides were broken. The only open rides were so crowded, and the lines were horribly long. We asked to speak to a manager, but no one knew where the idiot was. Even the food at the snack bar was lame. For these reasons, I would like to request a ticket price refund. I have enclosed our ticket stubs in this envelope.

1. Underline the sentences that use an inappropriate tone for a business letter. What words or phrases make these sentences inappropriate? _____

_____

2. Choose two of the inappropriate sentences and rewrite them to be more fitting for a business letter.

_____

_____

3. What is the purpose of this letter? _____

_____

4. What action does the writer want the recipient to take?

_____

5. What else would the recipient expect to find enclosed with this letter? Why?

_____

_____

Imagine you had an outstanding experience at the same adventure park. On another sheet of paper, write a short business letter that provides information about your experience.

For additional help, review pages 304–307 in your textbook or visit www.voyagesinenglish.com.

Chapter 3 • 149

Adjective and Adverb Clauses

An **adjective clause** modifies a noun or a pronoun. An **adverb clause** modifies a verb, though it can also modify an adjective or another adverb.

Underline the adjective clause or the adverb clause in each sentence, and circle the word or phrase it modifies. Write *adjective* or *adverb* to identify each.

1. My brother, who is an expert skier, enjoyed your snowboard terrain park. _____

2. I had saved my hard-earned money so that I might buy this laptop. _____

3. Mr. Eugene Olson was the person who directed us to you. _____

4. My old computer worked, although some of the keys were missing. _____

5. It was lunchtime at the lodge, which explains why it was so crowded. _____

6. Our admission to the museum was free because it was a Tuesday. _____

7. The program, which I only recently purchased, failed to reboot. _____

8. We left the ticket booth after our money had been refunded. _____

Rewrite each sentence by adding an adjective clause to modify the italicized noun. Circle the relative pronouns in your sentences.

9. Your *staff* provided every luxury we desired.

   _____

10. The *hotel* was more beautiful than we ever imagined.

   _____

11. I am available to speak with you at any *time*.

   _____

Rewrite each sentence by adding an adverb clause to modify the italicized words. Circle the subordinate conjunctions in your new sentences.

12. We *weren't feeling* very hungry.

   _____

13. The product *should be replaced*.

   _____

14. You *can watch* the game.

   _____

© Loyola Press. Voyages in English   Grade 8

For additional help, review pages 308–311 in your textbook or visit www.voyagesinenglish.com.

LESSON 4

Compound Words and Clipped Words

Compound words are made up of two or more shorter words. **Clipped words** are shortened versions of longer words.

Complete each sentence with the correct form of the compound word.

1. The (data base   database) for their online marketing efforts is very thorough.

2. This documentary was a real (eyeopener   eye-opener).

3. The former (vice-president   vice president) made the film about the environment.

4. He gave a lot of (forethought   fore thought) to what he was about to say.

5. The (book mobile   bookmobile) has many references for information about birds.

6. The (wingspan   wing span) of an albatross is enormous.

7. The banquet honored the contributions of several TV news (anchor women   anchorwomen).

Write the plural form of each compound word.

8. anchorman _____   11. five-year-old   _____

9. sister-in-law _____   12. lieutenant colonel _____

10. checkmark _____   13. passerby   _____

Write the longer form of each clipped word and the clipped form of each longer word.

14. fridge _____   20. math   _____

15. stats _____   21. preparatory _____

16. combination _____   22. flu   _____

17. grad _____   23. draperies   _____

18. tie _____   24. rhino   _____

19. laboratory _____ 25. professional _____

Use the form of each word in a sentence appropriate for a business letter.

26. gym _____

27. zoo _____

28. memo _____

29. typo _____

30. vet _____

For additional help, review pages 312–315 in your textbook
or visit www.voyagesinenglish.com.

Writing Tools

A **summary** is a condensed version of a text written in your own words.
Paraphrasing restates the same details of a text in a new way. **Plagiarizing**
is taking someone else's words or ideas and presenting them as your own.

**Read each passage. Identify the text that follows as a *summary*, a *paraphrase*, or
plagiarism. Explain your answer.**

1. **Passage:** *Pirates of the Caribbean* is a movie written by Ted Elliott and Terry Rossio. The
story's conception was based on the Pirates of the Caribbean ride at Disney Theme Parks.

_____ Writers Ted Elliott and Terry Rossio got the idea for the movie *Pirates of
the Caribbean* from the Disney Theme Park ride of the same name.

_____

2. **Passage:** Poor conditions, crowded cities, and unarmed supply ships are three major
causes for piracy on the high seas.

_____ Poor conditions, very crowded cities, and supply ships that were
unarmed are three causes for piracy on the high seas.

_____

3. **Passage:** During the Revolutionary War, the colonies did not have a navy that could face
the powerful British fleet. The American forces instead hired privateers, pirate ships hired to
do battle against British warships. Without these privateers, the American colonies may not
have had a chance of success against the powerful British navy.

_____ Privateers were pirates for hire that actually helped the American
colonies win the Revolutionary War.

_____

On another sheet of paper, summarize the following passage.

4. Legend says that the pirate Edward Teach, also known as Blackbeard, left 15 mutineers on
an island with only a bottle of rum and a sword. This island is small, rocky, and treeless with
high cliffs and no potable water. Survival here would have been impossible. The island is now
called Deadman's Chest.

On another sheet of paper, paraphase the following passage.

5. The ship glided down the channel with only one sail flying in the wind. The captain and crew
had just crossed the Atlantic Ocean from Africa. They were now in the British Virgin Islands,
but they couldn't relax just yet. After violent storms just two days before, they wanted to
secure the vessel and its cargo before heading to shore.

For additional help, review pages 316–319 in your textbook
or visit www.voyagesinenglish.com.

What Makes a Good Description?

> **Descriptive writing** uses vivid language to bring to life a person, a place, a thing, or an idea. Descriptive writing can be objective or subjective but should create a detailed picture in a reader's mind.

Read the descriptive paragraph. Then answer the questions.

The kitchen was the heart and soul of Ana's home. This was where Ana's mama prepared love for all to share. Ana sat quietly on her stool and watched Mama move about the kitchen. Mama's slender fingers were a blur as she chopped, grated, and sliced. In her skilled, caring hands, food wasn't cooked; it was created. She didn't prepare dishes; she created masterpieces. Mama moved gracefully around the kitchen like a dancer, her long skirt swishing softly around her legs. Ana watched as Mama grated fresh nutmeg into a bowl of creamy sauce. The warm air almost burst with the fragrances of fresh herbs and hot spices. Boiling sauces popped softly on the stove, while onions, garlic, and peppers sizzled in a pan. Ana's mama looked up and smiled. Ana knew that one day she would dance in the kitchen, just like her mama.

1. What is the mood of this passage? Why do you think so?

   _____

   _____

2. What words does the writer use to help you see, smell, and hear what is happening?

   I see _____ .

   I smell _____ .

   I hear _____ .

3. How does this passage make you feel? Why?

   _____

Rewrite each sentence by adding sensory details.

4. The snow was cold in my hands.

   _____

5. Our celebration was interrupted by rain.

   _____

For additional help, review pages 338–341 in your textbook or visit www.voyagesinenglish.com.

Chapter 4 • 153

Organization

Good descriptive writing organizes details in a meaningful way. Descriptive writing can be organized by **chronological order, spatial order, order of importance,** or **comparison and contrast.**

Read the descriptive paragraph and answer the questions.

> Maui and Leah are quite different. Being twins, you'd think they would be similar, but it's just not true. Maui is a natural artist. She loves to create with her hands through painting and sketching. Leah is a natural athlete. She'd rather swing a tennis racquet than sit in front of a sketch pad. Both girls, however, enjoy riding horses and going to the beach.

1. How is this passage organized? _____

2. How do you know? _____

_____

Write the method of organization you might use for each topic. Then list ideas for details you might include in a descriptive paragraph about each topic.

3. a perfect winter day _____

_____

4. the final hectic days of a family vacation _____

_____

5. the best and the worst movie you saw last summer _____

_____

6. a list of ways to recycle at home _____

_____

Identify the method of organization used in each statement.

7. About the only thing my new school had in common with my old one is that they were both buildings. _____

8. Once inside the front door, climb the ornately carved staircase as your fingers trace the handrail, worn smooth by those who have lived here. _____

9. Exhausted, I dropped my luggage and sat heavily on the bed, the fantastic events of the previous week replaying in my head. _____

10. Most important of all, they knew it was crucial that the fire be put out completely before they left the campsite. _____

For additional help, review pages 342–345 in your textbook or visit www.voyagesinenglish.com.

LESSON
3

Graphic Organizers

The right **graphic organizer** can help map out and organize details for descriptive writing. A **Venn diagram** compares and contrasts two items or ideas, while a **word web** helps organize details in a variety of ways.

Read each description. Write whether it best describes a *Venn diagram*, a *word web*, or *both*.

1. helps writers consider similarities and differences _____

2. can be used to sort and eliminate less important details _____

3. may help organize details for a spatial description _____

4. used by writers to organize and sort details for descriptive writing _____

5. allows writers to weigh comparisons of two topics _____

6. permits writers to brainstorm a variety of details for a description _____

Use the Venn diagram to compare and contrast details that describe your favorite indoor place and your favorite outdoor place.

7.

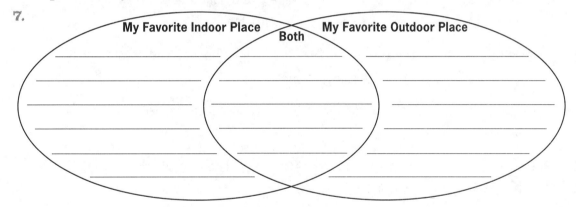

My Favorite Indoor Place   Both   My Favorite Outdoor Place

Write whether you would use a Venn diagram or a word web to organize details for each topic question. Explain your choice.

8. How did the construction of the transcontinental railroad change the way people lived?

_____

9. What points of interest should a tourist see on a visit to Yosemite National Park?

_____

10. Would a visit to an art festival or a museum be a better choice for a class field trip?

_____

11. Which species of insects live in colonies, and what are these colonies like?

_____

For additional help, review pages 346–349 in your textbook or visit www.voyagesinenglish.com.

LESSON
4

Thesaurus

A **thesaurus** is a book of synonyms and related words. Some words have both **denotations,** or literal meanings, and **connotations,** or implied meanings. Use a dictionary to be sure a replacement word has the correct meaning.

Write at least three synonyms for each word. Use a thesaurus if needed.

1. try _____

2. happy _____

3. scared _____

4. get _____

Circle the word that is the best synonym for the underlined word in each sentence. Use a thesaurus if needed.

5. The rough seas made the trip to the island extremely uncomfortable.

    stumble   journey   crossing   outing

6. Teresa felt seasick from the pitching and rolling of the boat on the waves.

    unsettled   nauseous   indisposed   troubled

7. This year's boat show displayed the newest crafts in sailboating and powerboating.

    vocation   journey   vehicles   vessels

8. We dressed in our best formal clothes for the yacht club's annual ball.

    textiles   attire   costumes   disguises

9. The commodore greeted the guests warmly as they stepped inside the door.

    enthusiastically   carefully   warily   genuinely

Explain the differences in connotation between the words in each set. Use a dictionary if needed.

10. intimidated, anxious _____

    _____

11. crafty, astute _____

    _____

12. frail, delicate _____

    _____

13. notorious, famous _____

    _____

For additional help, review pages 350–353 in your textbook or visit www.voyagesinenglish.com.

LESSON
5   Figurative Language

Figurative language goes beyond the literal meaning of words. **Similes, metaphors, personification,** and **hyperbole** are examples of figurative language that can create vivid imagery in a reader's mind.

Underline the two things being compared in each sentence. Then write whether the sentence is a *simile* or a *metaphor*.

1. My big black cat slithers around my ankles like a snake.   _____
2. The teacher is a hawk circling the classroom during exams.   _____
3. His skin was as rough as sandpaper after working in the sun.   _____
4. She is a graceful swan when she dances across the stage.   _____
5. This new computer is faster than the blink of an eye.   _____

Write hyperbole to complete each sentence.

6. The tree is so tall _____ .
7. That baby cries so much _____ .
8. It's so warm this summer _____ .
9. Yesterday's test was so hard _____ .
10. Dad's new watch was so expensive _____ .

Underline the personified noun in each sentence. Circle the word or words that give human qualities to the noun.

11. The sun snuggled below the horizon as it set at the end of the day.
12. With the coming storm, the wind howled through the trees.
13. My bed beckons to me when I am truly exhausted.
14. After a few hard shakes, the ketchup finally crawled out of the bottle.
15. A sudden gust made the autumn leaves dance and skip across the yard.
16. I felt the kiss of the warm summer breeze tickle softly on my cheek.

Use a simile, a metaphor, hyperbole, or personification to write a descriptive sentence for each topic.

17. a dog that constantly barks _____

_____

18. a huge wave at the beach _____

© Loyola Press. Voyages in English   Grade 8

For additional help, review pages 354–357 in your textbook or visit www.voyagesinenglish.com.

Chapter 4 • 157

What Makes a Good Expository Essay?

The purpose of an **expository essay** is to inform. An expository essay provides relevant information about a specific topic and often answers the questions *who*, *what*, *when*, *where*, *why*, and *how*.

Write a word to complete each statement.

1. The topic of an expository essay is clearly stated in the _____.

2. Order of importance, comparison and contrast, cause and effect, and chronological order are all forms of _____.

3. The conclusion _____ the main idea of the essay.

Read the passage and answer the questions.

The Declaration of Independence stated that the colonies in America were free from British rule, a revolutionary idea at the time. The colonists considered themselves free and independent and wanted to govern themselves as a new nation. They believed that all people have certain rights that cannot be taken away by a government or ruler. The ideas in the Declaration of Independence were considered so revolutionary that the British declared the document treasonous, and the Revolutionary War began. However, the desire for freedom helped the colonists defeat the British to win independence.

4. What is the topic of this essay? _____

5. What is the main idea? _____

6. What are some supporting details? _____

_____

_____

7. How does the concluding sentence sum up the main idea? _____

_____

Write a method of organization for each topic.

8. the specific sequence of launch procedures for the space shuttle _____

9. whether certain foods or supplements are better nutrient sources _____

10. a ranking of steps one can take to set up a home budget _____

© Loyola Press. Voyages in English   Grade 8

For additional help, review pages 376–379 in your textbook or visit www.voyagesinenglish.com.

LESSON
2

Fact and Opinion

Facts are statements that can be verified or proved true. **Opinions** are statements of judgment.

Write *fact* or *opinion* to identify each statement. Circle the opinion signal words.

1. It's evident that dogs are significantly easier to train than cats. _____
2. Mercury's orbit around the sun is shorter than that of Earth. _____
3. Certainly people who eat healthful foods live longer lives. _____
4. Thomas Jefferson signed the Declaration of Independence. _____
5. Our football team won the state championship last year. _____
6. Everyone knows that Mrs. Lila Davidson is a truly talented lawyer. _____
7. Being stranded with a flat tire is a dangerous situation. _____
8. The final game of the season will be held next week. _____

Write one fact and one opinion about each topic.

9. a book you have recently read

   Fact: _____

   Opinion: _____

10. a favorite food

   Fact: _____

   Opinion: _____

11. a hobby or craft

   Fact: _____

   Opinion: _____

On another sheet of paper, rewrite this persuasive essay to make it expository. Delete or revise opinions so the purpose of the essay is to inform.

Flying in the front seat of a small plane is so much fun. The engine roars to life, the plane speeds down the runway, and then at 90 mph, it lifts off the ground. Suddenly, you have a bird's-eye view of your town. Learning takes time, but it's easy. Forty hours of training earns you a license that allows you to fly the plane alone. Imagine that! Pilots can get great jobs flying for the airlines or private planes for companies or celebrities. Go take a test flight. Then give learning to fly a try.

For additional help, review pages 380–383 in your textbook or visit www.voyagesinenglish.com.

Chapter 5 • 159

LESSON
3

Evaluating Web Sites

The Internet is a source of information but not all these sources are reliable. **Evaluating Web sites** helps writers locate reliable sources and use the Internet safely.

Write the letter to match each description with a three-letter extension. Some extensions are used more than once.

1. a government site _____
2. a military site _____
3. site developed by a school or university _____
4. a commercial site _____
5. a site sponsored by an organization _____
6. a nonprofit group _____
7. a private business _____

a. .gov

b. .edu

c. .mil

d. .org

e. .com

Circle the two Web sites that would likely provide the most reliable information for each topic.

8. the number of cheetahs living in Africa
   - **a.** a pbs.org site on African wildlife
   - **b.** a .com site with an unknown sponsor
   - **c.** a .edu site of a prominent university
   - **d.** a .com site of a fur coat retailer

9. the meaning and history of your family's name
   - **a.** a .org site for name etymology
   - **b.** a .gov site for family name history
   - **c.** a name search site that charges a fee
   - **d.** a .com geneology site

10. the last five winners of the Oscar for Best Picture
    - **a.** a .org movie fan Web site
    - **b.** a .com site with a blog of movie trivia
    - **c.** a .org site for newspaper archives
    - **d.** the official site for the Academy Awards

11. important battles that turned the tide in the Civil War
    - **a.** a .com site of a Civil War hobbyist
    - **b.** a .gov site with a Civil War time line
    - **c.** a .edu site of a student report
    - **d.** a .edu site of American history

Make a list of topics you might type into a search engine to research information about aircraft used by the U.S. Navy during World War II.

_____

_____

For additional help, review pages 384–387 in your textbook or visit www.voyagesinenglish.com.

Noun Clauses

> A **noun clause** is a subordinate clause used as a noun. Noun clauses are usually introduced with words such as *how, whether, what, why,* and *that.*

Underline each noun clause. Write whether it is used as a *subject*, a *subject complement*, a *direct object*, an *object of a preposition*, or an *appositive*.

1. They couldn't decide whether they should stay or go.   _____

2. Why we can't visit Arkansas this summer is a mystery.   _____

3. The manual explains how the telescope is constructed.   _____

4. It is a verifiable fact that I read 15 books over the summer.   _____

5. I could see deer from where I was standing in the meadow.   _____

6. What we should make for dinner was up for debate.   _____

7. The problem was that we didn't have enough money.   _____

8. My dream, that I get the lead role, was finally realized.   _____

Write an appropriate noun clause to complete each sentence.

9. We were amazed _____.

10. Mother decided _____.

11. The fact _____ cannot be argued.

12. _____ is not open for debate.

13. The question is _____.

Use noun clauses to combine each pair of sentences into one sentence.

14. John declared. The party had started without us.

    _____

15. The dog keeps escaping from the yard. This issue is our problem.

    _____

16. All of us will attend the year-end field trip. That will be the reward.

    _____

17. The polling places have now closed. This has been reported.

    _____

18. The community has an excellent recycling program. Meyer wrote about this.

    _____

Prefixes

A **prefix** is a syllable or syllables placed at the beginning of a word to change
its meaning or to make another word.

**Underline the prefix in each group of words. Then using the information in the
box, write the meaning of each prefix.**

not	against	surpassing	too much	back/again
many/much	before	two	bad	between	one

1. illegal, illiterate, illogical   _____

2. interwoven, interaction, interchange   _____

3. biannual, biform, bicoastal   _____

4. antibacterial, antisocial, antiterrorist   _____

5. multifaceted, multipurpose, multimedia   _____

6. mistake, mismanage, misinform   _____

7. preplan, prenuptial, preorder   _____

8. outpace, outnumber, outrank   _____

9. overheated, overwrought, overemotional   _____

10. rematch, reiterate, reevaluate   _____

11. monolayer, monorail, monoculture   _____

**Underline the prefix in each word. Write the meaning of the word. Then write a
sentence using the word correctly.**

12. outdistance _____

_____

13. predetermined _____

_____

14. overestimated _____

_____

15. discontinue _____

_____

© Loyola Press. Voyages in English   Grade 8

For additional help, review pages 392–395 in your textbook
or visit www.voyagesinenglish.com.

LESSON
1

What Makes Good Persuasive Writing?

Good **persuasive writing** focuses on one topic and tries to convince readers to share the writer's viewpoint. Persuasive writing includes a position statement, reasons supporting the position, and a conclusion.

Write *P* (position), *S* (supporting), or *C* (conclusion) to identify the purpose of each sentence.

1. Everyone needs to eat fruits and vegetables. _____

2. If we want to keep our earth healthy for future generations, then it is important that we help clean the environment today, tomorrow, and every day hereafter. _____

3. Vitamin C is a highly effective antioxidant in humans. _____

4. One advantage is that this game allows children to get exercise. _____

5. Therefore, if you want to reduce the risk of certain diseases and provide for a healthier life, eat more fruits and vegetables. _____

6. Wind generators will start producing power at 7.5 mph wind speed. _____

Read the passage. Then answer the questions.

The Bengal tiger is disappearing at an alarming rate. Like other species that have been brought back from near extinction, this animal must be saved.

It is estimated that there are fewer than 3,000 Bengal tigers left in the wild. There are several reasons for this. The primary reason is that tigers are heavily hunted for sport, even though it is outlawed. Also, an increase in human population and farming has caused the tiger to lose large areas of natural habitat.

The human population continues to grow, and the tigers continue to disappear. It is imperative that we protect these beautiful animals.

7. What is the author's position statement?

_____

8. List one opinion and one fact that supports the author's position.

_____

_____

9. What is the author's conclusion?

_____

For additional help, review pages 414–417 in your textbook or visit www.voyagesinenglish.com.

© Loyola Press. Voyages in English   Grade 8

Chapter 6 • **163**

Voice and Audience

The tone of **voice** in a persuasive essay sets the mood. A writer chooses a particular voice or mood to persuade the **audience.**

Write words from the box that best describe the tone of voice required for each topic. Then write a position statement to reflect the mood.

angry	frank	enthusiastic	caring	concerned	funny

1. Topic: Convince the community to attend an open house for the Seaside Animal Shelter.

   _____

   _____

2. Topic: Speak out about taking a stand against animal cruelty.

   _____

   _____

Write a word from the box that best describes an appropriate tone to use for the audience of each topic. Then write an introduction for a persuasive essay.

3. You are applying for an after-school job at the community recreation center.

   _____

4. You believe the city council should consider building a skateboard park.

   _____

For each position statement, write a sentence that an active listener might argue if he or she disagreed with the statement.

5. After-school programs are a waste of time.

   _____

   _____

6. Art and athletic programs are important for a well-rounded education.

   _____

© Loyola Press. Voyages in English   Grade 8

For additional help, review pages 418–421 in your textbook or visit www.voyagesinenglish.com.

LESSON 3

Advertisements

The purpose of an **advertisement** is to persuade someone to buy or do something. Advertising is designed to appeal to the desires of its audience.

Write the propaganda device used in each statement. Then use the same device to write a persuasive statement about each new product.

> bandwagon   loaded words   testimonial   vague or sweeping generalities

1. Quarterback Jason Cooper claims, "Sore No More soothes all my aches and pains after a game." _____
   Shampoo: _____

2. Give these cuddly, homeless kittens a safe, warm place to sleep at night.
   _____
   Zoo fund-raiser: _____

3. No other store in the city can give you a better deal on a portable media player.
   _____
   Car dealership: _____

4. Even actress Shania Stone uses White 'n' Bright whitening toothpaste.
   _____
   Sports drink: _____

5. Everyone who's anyone loves *Shakespeare in the Park*. _____
   Movie: _____

6. Jake's Barbeque makes the best ribs in town. _____
   Summer carnival: _____

Write *credible* or *not credible* to evaluate each advertising statement. Circle the claim and underline the supporting detail if credible.

7. This computer has lightning speed due to its 5 TB hard drive. _____

8. This year the largest carnival in the world comes to town. _____

9. Our football team is the best in the league because of this year's undefeated record. _____

10. All the kids love Lulu's spinach roll-ups. _____

11. This SUV is preferred by every sports enthusiast. _____

For additional help, review pages 422–425 in your textbook or visit www.voyagesinenglish.com.

Chapter 6 • 165

Transition Words

Transition words and phrases connect one idea to the next. These connections help writing flow and make it easier to understand.

Circle the transition word or phrase that correctly completes each sentence.

1. Justin gave his speech to the audience, (while   in addition) Tara waited behind the curtain.

2. Katie held up the advertising sign (in front of   therefore) the new farmer's market.

3. All of us will make it to the game (but   unless) it starts to snow again.

4. Jennifer wouldn't enter her painting in the show (furthermore   because) she felt it wasn't good enough.

5. (However   Unlike), the books will continue to be on sale until Thursday.

6. Jamie wants to go to summer camp; (to begin with   on the other hand), he has an offer for a great part-time job.

7. The Strawberry Festival is lots of fun; (furthermore   therefore), it has the biggest Ferris wheel in the state.

8. (In addition   Before), the hospital needs more volunteers to help with patient care.

9. Bailey stored the boxes in the attic (unless   behind) Grandpa's big trunk.

10. Tyler practiced all summer long, (yet   while) he still didn't make the basketball team.

For each topic write a persuasive sentence that uses the transition word or phrase in parentheses.

11. not completing a homework assignment (consequently)

_____

12. a difficult project (however)

_____

13. election results (as a result)

_____

Write a sentence that fits the idea of the transition that follows.

14. _____

unless something is done to improve drivers' awareness.

15. _____

on the other hand, the show was very entertaining.

For additional help, review pages 426–429 in your textbook or visit www.voyagesinenglish.com.

LESSON
5

Suffixes

A **suffix** is a syllable or syllables added to the end of a word to change its meaning or to make another word. The word to which the suffix is added is called the base word.

Underline each word that has a suffix. Then write the definition of the word.

1. The skier raced down the steep hill. _____

2. He quickly turned to maneuver around the gate. _____

3. His involvement in this race was special. _____

4. After rehabilitation the man is skiing again. _____

5. He's shown us that he's back as a competitor. _____

Write an appropriate suffix for each word. Then write the meaning of the new word and use it in a sentence.

6. responsible _____

7. thought _____

8. conduct _____

9. bold _____

10. assure _____

Write a word to correct the sentence by adding a suffix to each italicized word.

11. Some people want to *legal* a faster speed limit _____

12. It is my *responsible* to take out the trash every night. _____

13. After winning the writing contest, Maya felt *joy*. _____

14. Our class collected donations for the *home* shelter. _____

15. My sister Sara wants to be a *paint*. _____

16. You will need to *active* the alarm before you leave. _____

17. Please request that Jake get some *assist* with these boxes. _____

18. Jordan fell *exhausted* onto the grass after the hike. _____

19. A judge attempted to settle their *disagree*. _____

20. Her expression made her *sad* apparent. _____

21. The pile of leaves served to *soft* her tumble onto the lawn. _____

22. At the end of the play, the lead *act* took a deep bow. _____

For additional help, review pages 430–433 in your textbook
or visit www.voyagesinenglish.com.

LESSON
1

What Makes Good Playwriting?

Playwriting is a unique form of writing that is meant to be performed. All plays share the same parts: plot, theme, characters, setting, dialogue, and stage directions.

Read this excerpt from a play. Then answer the questions.

HANNAH: *(straggling behind the others)* This is crazy, you guys.

MATT: *(turning to Hannah)* Then why are you here? You've doubted this story all along, yet you still wanted to tag along.

ANDY: *(kneels between a rock and tree)* I think this is the spot. Look. *(unfolds a tattered piece of paper and shows others)*

TERRI: The map shows a tree and a rock just like this!

HANNAH: Oh, sure. This is the only rock and tree around here.

MATT: Just ignore her. Let's see if our detective work has paid off.

(Hannah retreats to downstage right and begins kicking at the grass. The others begin digging. A metallic clink indicates a shovel making contact with an object. The diggers kneel around the hole.)

ANDY: *(awestruck)* Wow!

(Hannah looks in the direction of the others.)

TERRI: Well, we never expected that, did we?

1. What is most likely the setting for this play? What details lead to that conclusion?

   _____

   _____

2. Would this scene most likely be the exposition, the rising action, or the falling action? Why?

   _____

   _____

3. What parts of the play gives clues about Hannah's character?

   _____

   _____

4. What might be a possible theme for this play?

   _____

   _____

© Loyola Press. Voyages in English   Grade 8

For additional help, review pages 452–455 in your textbook or visit www.voyagesinenglish.com.

LESSON
2

Play Structure and Format

All play scripts follow similar **structures** and **formats**. Plays are usually divided into acts, each of which may contain separate scenes. One-act plays are shorter and have simpler plots and fewer characters than multi-act plays.

Write a word or a phrase to complete each sentence.

1. Actors know where and how to move by following the _____.

2. The _____ provides information about each character.

3. A _____ gives information about the play's time and place.

4. The _____ is the only text in the script that is spoken.

5. _____ are from the perspective of the actor facing the audience.

Read this script. Then answer the questions.

> **JOHN:** (*calling out from offstage*) Sandy! Lee! Sparky! Where are you?
>
> **SANDY:** (*waving*) Over here! Sparky's found a raccoon!
>
> **LEE:** (*restraining a barking dog on a leash*) Hey, Sparky! Settle down.
>
> **JOHN:** (*running to center stage*) What is it, boy? What are you bark—
>
> **SANDY:** Oh no! Catch Sparky!

6. How can you tell the stage directions from dialogue? What do the stage directions tell?

   _____

   _____

7. What is the purpose of the dash in the dialogue?

   _____

Write a stage direction where indicated to provide action for this dialogue.

> **HEATHER:** These flowers smell so wonderful. Here, smell.
>
> _____
>
> **IAN:** Mmmm, they're very fragrant. What kind are they?
>
> **HEATHER:** They're lilacs. They're blooming now. Let me show you.
>
> _____
>
> **IAN:** I wondered what that shrub was.
>
> _____

For additional help, review pages 456–459 in your textbook
or visit www.voyagesinenglish.com.

LESSON
3

Dialogue, Monologue, and Asides

Dialogue is the spoken words of the characters. A **monologue** is a long speech given by one character. An **aside** is dialogue in which an actor stops the play's action and directly addresses the audience.

Answer each question.

1. What does carefully constructed dialogue add to a play?

   _____

   _____

2. What should dialogue be like if it is to sound like natural speech?

   _____

   _____

   _____

3. What is the difference between a monologue and a soliloquy?

   _____

   _____

Read the following dialogue. Write an aside for each character.

      MEGAN: Jeff! That's my tape recorder. Go get your own!

   _____

      JEFF: My batteries are dead. I need to use yours.

   _____

      MEGAN: No. Just get new batteries from the basement.
      JEFF: I don't have time. Let me use yours . . . please?

Write a soliloquy that either Megan or Jeff delivers to the audience, which relates to the previous dialogue.

_____

_____

_____

_____

© Loyola Press. Voyages in English   Grade 8

For additional help, review pages 460–463 in your textbook or visit www.voyagesinenglish.com.

Idioms, Slang, and Jargon

An **idiom** is a phrase whose literal meaning differs from the actual meaning. **Slang** is nonstandard, informal language. **Jargon** is the special vocabulary of a particular profession or hobby.

Use a phrase from the box to complete each line of dialogue. Each line comes from a different play, so use the context of the sentence to figure out your answer.

boom swings over the aft deck	lend a hand	in over your head
rubbed him the wrong way	mellow out	ollie that four set
see eye to eye	sit tight	

1. **PERCIVAL:** *(disgustedly)* I thought you were my biggest supporter, but now I can understand that we no longer _____.

2. **MOTHER:** *(turns to Dora)* Here, let me _____. This won't be such a chore with both of us doing it.

3. **CAPTAIN:** *(shouting loudly)* Comin' about. Look alive, mates. Mind your skulls as the _____.

4. **PROFESSOR:** *(pompously)* Are you sure medicine is the right degree for you? You failed your midterm exam, and your lab results are less than satisfactory. I do believe you are _____.

5. **HIPPIE:** Hey, _____. Me and my lady see how uptight you are, man.

6. **LT. NELSON:** Soldiers, _____ while I scout over the next bluff. Count to 20, then charge over the bluff with everything you've got.

7. **BUD:** *(in disbelief)* Did you see the way Rudy looked at me? Wow, somehow I must have _____.

8. **MATT:** *(takes off his helmet)* I thought I could _____, but I had to bail off the board at the last minute.

Write a definition for each idiom or slang expression.

9. beat around the bush _____

10. face time _____

11. back to square one _____

12. second thoughts _____

For additional help, review pages 464–467 in your textbook or visit www.voyagesinenglish.com.

Chapter 7 • 171

Free Verse

Free verse is a form of poetry that does not follow conventional rules of rhyme and rhythm. Its purpose is to evoke emotions and images.

Read the prose and the free verse passages below. Then answer the questions.

Dew is a deposit of tiny water droplets that form on surfaces when they cool to a temperature colder than the dew point of the air next to that surface. Water vapor condenses into a liquid and attaches to the exposed surfaces, such as grass and spider webs. Dew appears as tiny beads of water before the sun evaporates them back into vapor.

Dew shimmering, clings
Reflects what it sees
Air squeezed the cold from night
Flowers, grasses
Toys shiver
Wet with the morning sun

1. Which passage seems to be informative and which seems to be imaginary? Explain.

   _____

   _____

2. Does the poem give factual information? What pictures does the poem bring to mind?

   _____

   _____

3. Why is the poem considered free verse?

   _____

Write sensory images that might be used to represent each word.

4. sadness _____

5. satisfaction _____

6. soreness _____

7. freshness _____

8. heat _____

© Loyola Press. Voyages in English   Grade 8

For additional help, review pages 468–471 in your textbook or visit www.voyagesinenglish.com.

LESSON
1

What Makes a Good Research Report?

A good **research report** is a comprehensive piece of expository writing that has a clear focus. A thesis statement clearly states a single topic and is developed in the body of the report. A conclusion summarizes the thesis.

Read the passage. Then answer the questions.

Both hurricanes and tornadoes have historically shown themselves to be some of the most dangerous of severe weather phenomena. Consider these two storms: To date, the most destructive tornado on record occurred in 1925—the Tri-State Tornado. It traveled 219 miles, damaging three states in its path: Missouri, Illinois, and Indiana. Although technology wasn't available to measure wind speed at the time, today we know that a tornado's winds can reach up to 300 miles per hour. Just like tornadoes, the destructive force of a hurricane is also caused by high winds. One of the most destructive on record occurred in 2005. With winds measuring over 175 miles per hour, Hurricane Katrina roared through southern Florida and strengthened to devastate parts of Louisiana, Mississippi, and Alabama. An estimated $75 billion in damage was reported.

1. What is the author's thesis?

_____

2. How did the author organize the paragraph?

_____

3. What types of factual information does the author use to support the thesis?

_____

_____

Circle the answer that best narrows each topic for a research report.

4. computer games

    a. new technology in computer games

    b. computer programming

    c. games around the world

5. colleges

    a. colleges in the United States

    b. private versus public colleges

    c. the history of colleges

For additional help, review pages 490–493 in your textbook or visit www.voyagesinenglish.com.

Research and Organization

An important part of prewriting a research report is **research and organization.** Notes are gathered from various sources. Organizing the notes into an outline can then help develop a final thesis statement.

Circle the letters of the two choices that best complete each statement.

1. When taking notes,

    a. use one note card for all details and include each source's name and page number.

    b. write each detail on a separate note card and include source information.

    c. do not use direct quotations.

    d. write the reference information for each source on a separate set of cards.

2. When organizing notes,

    a. combine the note cards so you have just one main idea.

    b. remove any note cards that do not fit your thesis.

    c. arrange groups of note cards into a preliminary outline that best supports your thesis.

    d. do not adjust your thesis statement based on the details you have found.

3. When using an outline,

    a. follow a specific format.

    b. group your information into large categories with few details.

    c. sort main ideas into subtopics supported by details.

    d. do not rely on it to help you with the direction of your writing.

Classify each of these notes for a research report on the Statue of Liberty into subtopics by writing *time line, financing,* or *construction.* If a note does not fit any of these subtopics, write *eliminate.*

4. France gave this statue to the United States in 1885. _____

5. Frederic Auguste Bartholdi designed the sculpture. _____

6. The sculpture was to be finished in 1876 for the centennial of the Declaration of Independence. _____

7. France made advances in ironworking. _____

8. Completion was delayed due to lack of funds. _____

9. Constructed in parts so statue could be easily shipped. _____

10. Lotteries, benefits, and auctions raised money for the project. _____

11. Statue was finally dedicated on October 28, 1886. _____

12. The Eiffel Tower is an immense structure of iron latticework. _____

For additional help, review pages 494–497 in your textbook or visit www.voyagesinenglish.com.

© Loyola Press. Voyages in English Grade 8

Citing Sources

Whenever a source is used in a research paper, it must be cited. As part of the report, a Works Cited page provides information about the sources used.

Write *encyclopedia, book, Web site,* or *periodical* to identify the source of each citation.

1. Tammet, Daniel. *Born on a Blue Day.* New York: Free Press, 2006. _____

2. Ramsey, Chad. "Here and Beyond." *Travel Journal*
   May 2009: 18–21. _____

3. Morrell, John. "Smart Irrigation." *Log Home Living* 11 Apr. 2009
   <www.loghome.com/smart_irrigations/articles/2979>. _____

4. "Virginia Beach." *The Columbia Encyclopedia,* 2008 ed. _____

5. Thomas, Shane L. "School Days" *Making Math Easy* 10 Aug. 2010
   <www.schooldays.org>. _____

6. "The American Revolution." *Encyclopaedia Brittanica,* 2009 ed. _____

7. Jones, Cherise, and Maggie Wright. "Voting on Election Day."
   Denver Gazette 22 Jan. 2011: 3–6. _____

8. Lopez, Elena, and Jon Ramos. *The General: George Washington.*
   Chicago: WordWorks Inc., 2005. _____

9. Zeb, Kelly. *Life and Times of Amos Thomas.* New York: Lifetime
   Publishing, 2006. _____

Circle the letter of the choice that best completes each statement.

10. Other possible information sources that also need to be cited include
    - **a.** interviews and sound recordings.
    - **b.** radio and television programs.
    - **c.** newspaper and journal articles.
    - **d.** all of the above.

11. Enclose the text of a Web address in
    - **a.** parentheses.
    - **b.** quotation marks.
    - **c.** angle brackets.
    - **d.** all of the above.

12. An entry for a periodical should include
    - **a.** the author's name.
    - **b.** the titles of the article and the periodical.
    - **c.** the article's date and page numbers.
    - **d.** all of the above.

13. Parenthetical notation is
    - **a.** paraphrasing a source in your report.
    - **b.** another way to credit a source.
    - **c.** directly quoting a source in your report.
    - **d.** all of the above.

© Loyola Press. Voyages in English   Grade 8

For additional help, review pages 498–501 in your textbook
or visit www.voyagesinenglish.com.

Reference Tools

Reference tools are book resources that can be used to locate information specific to the topic of a report.

Complete each sentence by writing a reference source from the box.

almanac	*The Reader's Guide to Periodical Literature*	
encyclopedia	atlas	biographical reference

1. Historically, farmers use a year's _____ to find information about weather patterns.

2. For a report on the Mississippi River, you might use an _____ to gather information about the river's course and the states the river passes through.

3. Use a _____ to find information about Winston Churchill.

4. The first tool most people use to find information on specific topics is the _____.

5. Information about up-to-date articles from magazine sources can be found in _____.

6. *Who's Who in America* is an example of a _____.

7. A source that is published every year and contains information ranging from population statistics to significant yearly events is known as an _____.

Write the research tool you would use to find each example.

8. the top-selling songs of 2010 _____

9. dates of Genghis Khan's reign _____

10. a recent article on cancer research _____

11. the life of Dr. Martin Luther King Jr. _____

12. annual rainfall numbers for Arizona _____

13. magazine articles on Italian cooking _____

14. mountainous regions in Argentina _____

15. the American Revolution _____

16. the basketball career of Michael Jordan _____

17. the political boundaries of Poland _____

© Loyola Press. Voyages in English   Grade 8

For additional help, review pages 502–505 in your textbook or visit www.voyagesinenglish.com.

LESSON
5

Multiple-Meaning Words

Some words have more than one literal meaning. Use context clues to determine the correct meaning of **multiple-meaning words.**

Circle the letter of the sentence in which the underlined word has the same meaning as the underlined word in the first sentence.

1. The captain climbed up to the <u>bridge</u> before the crew released the lines.

   a. That covered <u>bridge</u> looks beautiful surrounded by the fall colors.

   b. To <u>bridge</u> the gap that formed between them, he had to make things right.

   c. The controls for the ship are located on the <u>bridge</u>.

2. Turn on the porch <u>light</u> after dark.

   a. These boxes are <u>light</u> enough to carry upstairs.

   b. The <u>light</u> in the kitchen needs a new bulb.

   c. Terrance will <u>light</u> a fire so we can roast marshmallows.

3. Mr. Jameson got a parking ticket and consequently had to pay the <u>fine</u>.

   a. This is a <u>fine</u> example of an 18th-century manuscript.

   b. Some public libraries no longer charge their patrons a <u>fine</u> for late books.

   c. A very <u>fine</u> thread was all that held the button on the sweater.

4. The hen remained on the eggs for several days, and at last they began to <u>hatch</u>.

   a. After much thought he started to <u>hatch</u> a plan.

   b. Slide the <u>hatch</u> shut before water enters the boat.

   c. Once the astronauts were in their seats, the <u>hatch</u> was secured on the capsule.

Write two sentences for each word, each one using the word a different way.

6. bank

   _____

   _____

7. heel

   _____

   _____

8. jar

   _____

   _____

© Loyola Press. Voyages in English   Grade 8

For additional help, review pages 506–509 in your textbook or visit www.voyagesinenglish.com.

Chapter 8 • **177**